HOLIDAYS & CELEBRATIONS
THROUGH THE YEARS

REMINISCE

A *REMINISCE* BOOK

Copyright © 2022 RDA Enthusiast Brands, LLC
1610 N. 2nd St., Suite 102
Milwaukee, WI 53212-3906

All rights reserved. Unauthorized reproduction, in any manner, is prohibited.
Reminisce is a registered trademark of RDA Enthusiast Brands, LLC.

ISBN: 978-1-62145-861-6
Component number: 117300112H

We are committed to both the quality of our products and the service we provide to our customers. We value
your comments, so please feel free to contact us at TMBBookTeam@TrustedMediaBrands.com.

For more *Reminisce* products and information, visit our website: *www.reminisce.com*

Printed in U.S.A.

10 9 8 7 6 5 4 3 2 1

Text, photography and illustrations for *Holidays & Celebrations Through the Years* are based on articles
previously published in *Reminisce* magazine (*www.reminisce.com*).

FRONT COVER PHOTOS
Easter: Bob Grannis/Leila Grossman/Getty Images;
Thanksgiving: Hiroko Masuike/Getty Images;
Christmas: Keystone-France/Getty Images
COLORIZATION
Front cover, Easter and Christmas; pages 6, 42, 64, 118, 142, 190: Sanna Dullaway

204

22

151

CONTENTS

LET THE FUN BEGIN

W elcome to the party!
We hope you enjoy this selection of nostalgic holiday moments from the pages of *Reminisce*.

Delight in memories of New Year's excitement and childhood romances on Valentine's Day. See photos of crazy Mardi Gras parades, charming St. Patrick's Day cards and fancy Easter attire.

Patriotic celebrations will get you thinking of summer get-togethers with your own family. And don't miss the notable story from Wilma Hofheins on page 82. Her grandfather drove President Taft in an open-air carriage during a San Francisco parade!

Admire Halloween costumes that only a mother could love (or make), and read about the history of favorite trick-or-treat candies. You'll also recall hearty Thanksgiving feasts and revisit the magic of Christmas morning, and of sitting on Santa's knee asking for those special gifts. There's a photo gallery dedicated to meeting Santa starting on page 184.

Plus, relive the joy of birthday parties, weddings and more. This one-of-a-kind compilation is full of smiles and touching memories from the holidays and celebrations we all cherish.

The Editors of Reminisce *Magazine*

New Year's Flashbacks

Take a look at celebrations past, from unique countdowns to family gatherings in the basement. The party happens every year!

FIRST HIGHBALL

Her dad the bartender served it up straight.

The Schulers rang in the new year together. Alice is the little girl in both photos.

I loved the New Year's Eve parties my parents hosted for our family when I was a kid growing up in the 1950s in Floral Park, New York. Some of my fondest holiday memories revolve around those fabulous house parties, which started in the living room and later moved down to our newly finished basement.

My older cousins Rich and Freddie were in a garage band, and each brought their instruments— a saxophone and a guitar. Uncle Carl played the drums, which were also carried down the basement stairs, much to the confusion of our dog Poochie! And Aunt Martha completed the quartet with her accordion.

Mom, who had been in a band in her teens, sometimes sat in on the saxophone, and everyone took a turn playing drums. I was 6 years old and thought everyone had live music in the basement on New Year's Eve!

While the band played, Dad handled bartending duties. When I was old enough to stay up until midnight and saw everyone "ordering" drinks from him, I asked if I could have a highball.

Dad said, "Sure," and gave me a glass of ginger ale with a teaspoon of whiskey in it. I thought I was pretty grown up, and it tasted good, too! So I went back for another, and another, and another. After the first drink Dad gave me nothing but straight ginger ale. Everyone thought this was cute, until I went back to school and told my first-grade teacher that I'd had six highballs on New Year's Eve!

Alice Schuler • Floral Park, NY

Countdown to Quirky

Travel to places that make New Year's Eve distinct by dropping pies, pickles and watermelons at the stroke of midnight—or pretty close to it.

WATERMELON DROP

When the clock strikes midnight on New Year's Eve in Vincennes, Indiana, an 18-foot, 500-pound, cardboard-and-foam-covered steel watermelon descends from a crane in the sky. As it nears the ground, the giant melon opens, and watermelons from Knox County, Indiana, are dropped onto a large "splatform" as fireworks erupt. Indiana is home to more than 7,000 acres of watermelons. The New Year's Eve drop is a fun and festive tradition for our community to celebrate its agricultural heritage.

Loretta Day • Vincennes, IN

PICKLE DROP

On New Year's Eve, we drop papier-mache pickles into a barrel. At 7 p.m. (midnight in Ireland), a 16-inch-long pickle named Lil' Dill descends from the town's ladder firetruck. This early drop is a nod to Dillsburg's first settler, Irish immigrant Matthew Dill. Mr. Pickle, a larger 6-foot-tall version, lands in the barrel at midnight. Our town doesn't have a connection to pickles, but we sure love a good play on words.

Sharon Stauffer
Dillsburg, PA

MOONPIE DROP

On Dec. 31, Mobile, Alabama, celebrates Mardi Gras-style. Our Mardi Gras celebration is the oldest in the United States, making its debut here in 1703. The party includes a second line parade featuring a brass band and floats. MoonPies are thrown from the floats—an old Mardi Gras tradition—to a crowd of 50,000 people, and a 600-pound electric MoonPie drops from the side of a building at midnight. The night concludes with the cutting of the world's largest edible MoonPie, which weighs in at 154 pounds.

Michelle Browning • Daphne, AL

NEW YEAR'S 1946

The war was over, and relatives traveled across the country for a New Year's Eve gala in Elmwood Park, New Jersey. Everyone was invited—except us kids. I was exiled to Grandma's house with two cousins.

We normally had to go to bed after the *Lone Ranger* radio show at about 7:30, but Grandma said if we went to bed early, we could get up at midnight to celebrate (as long as we didn't wake her).

Too excited to sleep, I lay on Grandma's couch waiting for 12 bongs from her old clock shaped like a Roman soldier on a stool. It was like waiting for Christmas after Thanksgiving. Then it came.

I tiptoed upstairs to wake my cousins, but they slept like the dead. So, alone at midnight, I quietly blew my own horn. Outside, sirens blared, horns honked, guns fired and people cheered in the street. The commotion grew louder, then suddenly all was silent again. I returned to the couch and went to sleep, the Roman soldier standing guard on the mantel.

John E. Karp • El Mirage, AZ

A Whirlwind Tour

In my sophomore year at Ohio State, the Buckeyes beat the University of Michigan 12-10 to get to the Rose Bowl.

After Christmas, five of my buddies and I took a school-chartered flight to California and stayed with friends in Long Beach. We spent four days sightseeing at Disneyland, Las Vegas, Beverly Hills and Tijuana, Mexico. On New Year's Eve, we headed to the Ambassador Hotel on Wilshire Boulevard in Los Angeles, where the rest of the group was staying.

We toasted the new year twice, once at 9 p.m. in honor of Ohio time and again at midnight to honor local time. After downing several aspirin at 5:30 the next morning—New Year's Day 1975—we boarded a bus for the parade.

Then on to the Rose Bowl—what a sight! I was sitting at the base of the San Gabriel Mountains, and it was sunny and 71 degrees. And the game between OSU and the University of Southern California was exciting until the final minutes, when Ohio State lost 18-17 on a 2-point conversion by USC.

Bill Neuman • Pittsburgh, PA

Some of the family, including the dog, loved Aunt Bertha's meat loaf.

PUPPY LOVE

Please, no seconds or leftovers needed.

Aunt Bertha was known as a strict disciplinarian at the high school where she taught biology. Our family always found that pretty funny, because she had absolutely no control over her two kids or her pets at home!

In 1956, she hosted a memorable New Year's Day dinner. As always, she served her meat loaf, which Mom, Dad and Grandpa loved and my brother and I hated.

Shortly before we sat down to eat, Aunt Bertha took the meat loaf out of the oven and set the pan on the kitchen table. As soon as she walked away to get a spatula, the dog reached up with its front paws and pulled the pan to the floor.

Aunt Bertha screamed and rushed over to the pooch. I thought she was going to chew her out, but nope! She was afraid the pan had hit the dog and hurt her.

Once she saw that her pup was fine, she picked up the meat loaf from the floor, wiped it off and served it! I think that was our last New Year's meal at Aunt Bertha's house.

Nancy White • Omaha, NE

TIME MARCHES ON

Clocks ring in the new year.

OLDE-TYME ACCURATE

Telechron had been a venerable name in timepieces since 1923, when clock wizard Henry Ellis Warren trademarked it. Though once seen as chic, by the late '40s Telechrons were known more for accuracy than aesthetics. This model, with curtain-look casing and doubled numbers, appears stuck in an art deco time warp.

'47

'55

UPDATED LOOK

GE had steady earnings for years from its controlling interest in clockmaker Telechron, but slowing sales signaled a need for change. Its designer line in the mid-1950s jazzed up the look of the clocks, but sales didn't exactly ring any bells. GE ended the designer series in 1959. Many of the styles, including those shown, are collectible now.

Big Ben. The clock that has been waking people up for the past 60 years is introducing some eye openers.

For 60 years, our goal in life was to get people up on time. And for 60 years, nobody, but nobody, has done it better than us.

But times change. And, so do people's tastes in styles. Today, people want today's kind of look. Even in their alarm clocks.

At Westclox, we're giving it to them. What we've done is transplanted what many people have come to call the "world's most dependable ticker" into these young attractive bodies.

We call it the Big Ben Futura. It's perfect for kids' rooms, family rooms, or modern kitchens.

And at $9.98*, you're going to find it a great-looking clock at a great price.
*Manufacturer's suggested retail price.

Westclox
A DIVISION OF GENERAL TIME
A TALLEY INDUSTRIES COMPANY

'73

BIG-TIME ADJUSTMENT

Introduced by Western Clock Manufacturing Co. in 1909, the Big Ben went through several style changes over its long history, notably by industrial design guru Henry Dreyfuss, who did at least three iterations between 1931 and 1949. The Futura shown here was styled for kids' rooms and hip kitchens.

3, 2, 1—Happy New Year!

When we were kids in the '50s, we were never allowed to stay up late. But when I was 8, Mom told my older sister and me that Dad would be working late on New Year's Eve, so we could stay up with her and watch the late show. She made popcorn and Kool-Aid. The excitement built as we watched TV and waited—we had never stayed up that late before! A movie came on at 11, and all we had to do was wait one more hour. The next thing I remember, Mom was waking us up from the sofa and telling us to go to bed. My sister and I had slept through midnight! Now that I am in my 60s, I still sleep through it.

Carolann Ellmore

I remember that my parents would stay up just to hear the Guy Lombardo band play "Auld Lang Syne."

Charlene Phelps

My parents listened to my father's shortwave radio to hear Big Ben in London chime in the new year on Greenwich Mean Time. They were fast asleep long before anything happened in Times Square.

Charles Edwards III

"In 1969, I went on a blind date to a New Year's Eve party at the
Playboy Club in Denver. No idea now of the guy's name,
but I do remember that silk dress—I loved it."

Sandra Hubbs Wilmoth • Evans, CO

Valentine's, Mardi Gras and St. Patrick's Day Fun

Those heart-shaped greetings can be memorable—and the
Big Easy and the luck of the Irish bring out a festive spirit.

One-Room Schoolhouse Valentines

Valentine's Day is one of my favorite holidays—I'm a very sentimental person. Here are some of my valentines from the 1940s when I attended elementary school in a rural one-room schoolhouse. I received them from my cousins and very good friends. I still have those friends, but we're all much older now!

We would buy valentines at the five-and-dime store, where they had 2-by-2-foot glass bins full of them. One bin had nickel valentines, which were very pretty; other bins held smaller ones that were two or three for 5 cents. We didn't have very much money, so I would decide which valentines I could afford to buy with my allowance.

In those days, this was very important to us—oh my, it was just such a big deal! These valentines have always meant a lot to me, and that's why I've saved them.

Ardella Score • *Minot, ND*

CANDY KISSES

The love of her sixth-grade life gave her
a gift that melted her heart.

Back in the dark ages, when I was an 11-year-old sixth grader in Ms. Daisy Blogg's classroom, the most wonderful thing happened. I fell in love. It was magical as Buddy O'Toole and I zinged whimsical grins across four rows of desks.

I was tall for my age and just about as gangly as they come, while Buddy was short and just about as round as they come. But it hardly mattered, for nearly all the boys were shorter than the girls. My mother assured me I was experiencing puppy love, and that Buddy was just slow shedding his baby fat.

Thoughts of chocolates and surprises preoccupied me as Valentine's Day drew near. I could barely wait to hear what our teacher had planned as our tall classroom windows glittered with familiar sweet red angels and assorted paper hearts.

"Please bring a decorated container with your name clearly marked on the outside," Ms. Blogg announced. "You will make enough valentines for every box."

While the ladies fancied exchanging valentine greetings, the sixth-grade boys were not as sold on the custom, as it suddenly seemed juvenile, silly and mushy. Regardless, Buddy told me to make sure my container was at least as big as a shoebox. That day would be my first experience on cloud nine.

Walking to school, none of us escaped the cloudburst and squall swirling about the playground as we ran for cover with our valentines. The swings and trapezes banged and twirled, snarling their chains around and around. Then there was a sudden lull while they untangled at breakneck speed.

After placing our wet valentine boxes on the windowsills above the radiators, we spent the morning glancing at our wrinkled and fading handiwork. Ribbons and string hung limply, leaving strange arrays of bleeding pigments and hues upon all they touched. Nonetheless, for the girls the day dragged on endlessly.

As Ms. Blogg read aloud to us about the history of Valentine's Day, a sudden *psst, psst, psst* emanated from the radiator. We all broke out in giggles as we watched chocolate drip, drip, dripping from a corner of the big red shoe box marked "Kathleen." I glanced over at Buddy, but there were no smiles or giggles, just horror written all over his face. Buddy had spent all his allowance on Hershey's Kisses and meticulously pasted each one upon a card.

Finally, the 3 o'clock bell rang and the day was over. The students gathered their valentines under their coats for the drizzly trek home. I caught up with Buddy in the hall and asked him to meet me across the street at the library.

After choosing a corner spot, I set the table with his lovely chocolate-covered card and the knurly candy kisses. We sat and talked until a grin crossed Buddy's chubby cheeks, then we finished off the remains of a valentine that neither of us ever forgot.

Kathe Campbell • Butte, MT

Cupid Has an Off Day

A grade school declaration of love falls on eager ears.

VALENTINE—YOU'VE RUN AWAY WITH MY HEART!

By the time the dismissal bell rang at Central School in Wakefield, Michigan, in the mid-1940s, some students already had put away their valentines. I was surprised to find that one more had been left on my desk.

The greeting-card-style valentine was unsigned; stuck to the back was a note with its edges pasted shut. I didn't fully comprehend that this meant its contents were private. I loosened the white notepaper from the card and unfolded it, thinking that the mysterious sender might have signed it.

My friends Becky and Elaine watched with wide eyes. "That must be a real love letter!" Becky said.

I smiled. "You've been watching too many love stories! It's a valentine—not a love letter!"

Some boys overheard my too-loud answer and rushed over to find out what we were discussing. Expecting to find "Happy Valentine's Day," I opened the note and started to read in a whisper. Surprised by the message, my words increased in volume, just as it dawned on me that the message was personal and not meant as public news!

The message from my classmate Sam said: "I love you. Do you love me? Tell me sometime."

Several students gasped and some smiled. Sam ran out of the classroom.

I wished I'd known better than to open the valentine in front of anyone—now I had embarrassed Sam and I felt sick at heart. I followed him into the hall and said, "Sam, thank you for the note. Have a nice Valentine's Day!" He only nodded and shrugged.

As time passed, Sam and I became friends, and remembering that day gave us both a little laugh. But we never dated—romance had no chance after that fifth-grade love letter.

Audrey Carli • *Iron River, MI*

Cute valentines exchanged in Audrey's classroom inspired one little romantic.

THE 'NO' GIRL SAYS YES

True love happens when you least expect it.

Valentine's Day holds a special place in Jack's heart. That's when he met his wife-to-be, Marilyn.

Home from the Navy in 1947, I started school at Greenville College in my hometown of Greenville, Illinois. I had been out of high school for four years, but my high school principal, Mr. Gardner, invited me to a Valentine's Day dance at school. We lived in a small community, and the thought of seeing my former teachers was intriguing. So I agreed.

When Friday came, I gussied up and drove to the high school gym. I chatted with my former teachers and approached Mr. Gardner to thank him before leaving. Just then, the band started playing and a young woman stood up to sing. One look at her and I was mesmerized. I had never seen such a beautiful woman, so I concluded she was from a nearby town.

I asked Mr. Gardner who she was, and he said, "That's Marilyn Riley, Cut Riley's daughter."

I was flabbergasted to say the least. The Rileys lived just around the corner from me.

I walked across the gym floor to introduce myself and said, "Hi, I'm Jack Joseph."

"I know who you are," was her not-too-friendly response.

"Would you like to dance?" I asked.

"No!" she shot back.

"Why not?"

"I'm working," she replied.

"Can I call you next week for a movie date?"

"No," was her response.

I could see no reason to argue, so I thanked her for nothing, tucked my pride in my coat pocket and left.

For the next month I phoned, trying to set up a date. She always had the same answer: No.

Then one rainy afternoon in March as I was driving home after basketball practice, I saw Marilyn, the "No" girl, walking with no umbrella.

I pulled alongside her and asked if she needed a ride, half expecting her to say no. Instead, she stepped over the curb and plopped down on the seat next to me. It was only a few blocks to her house, but after pulling into her driveway we talked for 45 minutes. It was magic from then on.

Jack Joseph • Scottsdale, AZ

She Got Their Votes

On Valentine's Day 1946, I attended a dance at the Naval Air Station in Jacksonville, Florida. I wore a long pink gown to the event, where each of us girls received a corsage of red roses.

The servicemen voted for the prettiest girl to become Miss Valentine. After the votes were counted, the judges narrowed the list to 10 girls—and I was one of them.

When the judges announced the winner, they called my name! The band started playing as I walked through a giant valentine to dance with a Navy man before the crowd. I shall always cherish that night.

Jean Raynor • Richmond, VA

ROSES ARE RED-HANDED

Because I lived in the far reaches of the country in the early '50s, Valentine's Day posed a problem for me: As a fifth grader with no money or transportation, how was I to get my crush the valentine she deserved?

Luckily, my married sister, Jane, always made a trip home to bring my brothers and me nice valentines. While admiring a past year's card, I was struck with a brilliant idea.

After everyone had gone to bed on Valentine's eve, I found my card from Jane, carefully erased my name, and printed my beloved's name over the smudges. The next morning, I slipped the card into the box on the teacher's desk. The big moment arrived, and the teacher called the names one by one. I watched intently as my crush opened her card. I will never forget the look of bewilderment on her face when she read it. Her hand flew into the air. "Teacher," she asked, "why does mine say, 'Love, Jane & Richard?'"

Billy Cotner • Jackson, TN

HIS HEART WAS IN THE RIGHT PLACE

My brother John had just returned after serving in the military in World War II. While waiting for a permanent job he had been promised, he took on a few odd jobs for family and friends. Around the neighborhood he became known as Mr. Fixit.

It was February when he started a project to paint the interior of a house. The owner was a young widow named Cathy, a friend of a friend. As he painted, she went about her daily household chores and errands.

They would chat briefly or catch smiling glimpses of each other. He finally reached the last room to paint—the kitchen. Reluctantly, he put the finishing touches on his work. She brewed a pot of fresh coffee, and they both sat at the kitchen table while figuring the total expense of the paint job.

"It's a good thing I was off that ladder before I fell," he said with a teasing tone in his voice.

As she glanced about the room, she finally got the message. To her amazement, she saw a neat row of red hearts painted around the edge of the ceiling.

One large heart in the center was inscribed, "I love you!" It was Valentine's Day.

Ruth J. Anderson • Grove, OK

WAITING FOR PRINCE CHARMING

Her love arrived in an elevator on the sixth floor.

Looking down at the gift wrapped in heart-patterned paper, I smiled and held back tears. How many times would I find myself on Valentine's Day opening yet another gift from Mom, but not one from a beau?

I fastened the heart-shaped brooch from Mom to my lapel before leaving for work. Then I kissed her goodbye and joked, "I hope you have a lot of money. You're going to be stuck buying Valentine's gifts for me till the end of time."

"No, I won't," she said. "Your Prince Charming awaits. You just haven't noticed him yet. Make sure you're not wearing that sourpuss look on your face when he arrives."

Many months passed with no sighting of my Prince Charming. At least I hadn't seen him at Wanamaker's department store, where I worked as a secretary.

I often joked to co-workers about my lackluster social life. One day, as a friend and I rode a crowded store elevator, she announced, "Everyone, meet Annie. She's a whole lot of fun waiting to happen."

With that she got off on her floor and the elevator doors clapped shut. I turned scarlet.

A few days later my elevator stopped on the sixth floor and a young man named Joe stepped on. He looked at me and said, "Hi, Annie. I'll bet you're a lot of fun."

I laughed and said to him, "Oh, I guess you heard the announcement."

Our conversation ended there, but that wasn't the last I saw of Joe. He started sitting at my lunch table. Each day he moved one seat closer to me, until one day, just after lunch, he asked me if I would go out with him. I smiled and nodded yes.

For our first date, I wore a polka-dot sundress with a pink ribbon in my hair. I packed a picnic lunch for us, and later that evening we went to the movies.

Just as Mom predicted, I had found my Prince Charming. Joe and I have been married for decades now, and he still remembers what I wore on our first date.

Annmarie Tait • Conshohocken, PA

Annmarie and Joe goof around on their second date (far left). Married in 1984 (center), the Taits have celebrated many anniversaries together.

A SUGARY VALENTINE

Don't forget the chocolate!

MAKE IT A TWO-FER
The Whitman's Sampler became a staple in World War II, when the company shipped thousands of free boxes to troops overseas. By 1951, a Whitman's Sampler was the go-to treat for every occasion, from first dates to the last day of school. Or, in this case, from Valentine's Day to Easter.

CORDIALLY YOURS
Chicago-based Brach's was best known for its star-shaped chocolate candies, but its cherry cordials ran a close second. At one point, Brach's had the largest candy factory in the world. In the mid-1940s, its annual sales were $22 million.

Wouldn't you like some CANDY?

If you were a newspaper reporter and the presses were being held for your story and you had to keep on pounding it out and needed a quick energy pick-up, wouldn't *you* like some candy?

If you were an elevator starter and you wanted to produce a four o'clock treat for your friends around the building, what could be better than to say, "Wouldn't *you* like some *candy?*"

If you were the heartthrob of the prettiest girl in town, wouldn't it be swell to make your next "date" super special by saying, "Happy Valentine! Wouldn't *you* like some *candy?*"

CANDY IS DELICIOUS FOOD

Enjoy some every day!

COUNCIL ON CANDY of the NATIONAL CONFECTIONERS' ASSOCIATION
Headquarters: One North La Salle Street, Chicago 2, Illinois

te Cherries
finest!

Choice cherries—blessed with a rare blend of imported flavorings actually worth their weight in gold—are coated with Brach's rich chocolate! Only Brach's Chocolate-Covered Cherries have such out-of-this-world flavor!

BRACH uses only the finest cherries—treats them with maraschino syrup blended from imported flavorings to make this delicious candy. Then the cherries are given a generous benediction of vanilla creme triple-whipped to the velvet-smooth texture of whipping cream. And the coating is double-thick chocolate—made from selected cocoa beans carefully blended and ground in Brach's chocolate mills!

● You'll find Brach's Chocolate-Covered Cherries renowned for quality and flavor. For the family—for guests and for gifts—Brach's Chocolate-Covered Cherries are indeed the finest you can pick!

rach's
E CANDIES

'48

CANDY SWEETENS THE DEAL

Yes, once upon a time in America, the candy lobby advertised. This *Life* spot from the National Confectioners' Association shows the many ways candy can make things easier, whether you're banging out a breaking news story, persuading a girl to be your date or smoothing things over with the doorman.

Young Affections

Kid-friendly valentines for the whole class.

Boxes of die-cut cards with cute animals and silly wordplay became widely available in the baby-boom years. The packs had enough valentines for everyone, including the teacher, so no one would be left out.

My brother Edward received these valentines as a fifth grader at Monnier Elementary School in Detroit, Michigan, in 1950.

Robert Stewart • *Villa Rica, GA*

EVERYONE GOT MAIL!

As the smallest one on the playground, I loathed games like crack-the-whip. When the kids put me at the end of the whip line and then tore off across the playground, it was God's mercy I didn't land on the school roof.

Perhaps out of pity for my poor showing on the field, teachers chose me to make the valentine box for the class each year. I delighted in being chief engineer for the construction.

After school, my assistants helped me wrap the biggest cardboard carton we could find with crepe paper, leaving a slit in the top for the valentines. We covered it with red paper hearts and doilies and pictures cut from old valentines. Usually I walked to school, but our beautiful box was delivered in state—in Dad's car. I installed it at the rear of our classroom and reveled in admiring comments from my classmates.

Most kids brought valentines for every student, including the teacher. A great deal of thought went into selecting just the right sentiment for each classmate, especially for that special someone.

Millie Baker Ragosta
Bellefonte, PA

LET THE GOOD TIMES ROLL!

Carnival time in the Big Easy is like no other.

The Mardi Gras bug bit me back in 1959 when I was only 9 years old—thanks to the movie *Mardi Gras* starring Pat Boone and Christine Carère. Carère played the queen of the Mardi Gras parade, who wore a ballgown fit for a princess and threw strands of beads to the crowd. I decided then and there that someday I would come home with my own treasure trove of beads.

I finally made my Mardi Gras dreams come true in 2000. Having waited 41 years, I wanted the full experience. So my husband, Jim, and I took Amtrak's City of New Orleans train (which was decked out in gold, green and purple) from Chicago to the Big Easy. Once there, I was thrilled to learn that there was a parade that very night! Even with beads flying everywhere, my first catch was a plastic cup—now in a spot of honor on my bookshelf.

Throughout all the exquisite dining, shopping and sightseeing that followed, it was still all about the parades for me. With every procession that worked its way through the French Quarter, I threw my hands in the air, yelling: "Throw me some beads, mister!"

Finally I couldn't pile any more strands around my neck, so I focused on the high school bands and beautiful floats. So much effort went into entertaining visitors.

Jim and I were lucky enough to attend the Endymion Extravaganza, a formal ball held at the Superdome. (Endymion is one of Mardi Gras' "super krewes.")

The Endymion parade made several rounds within the Superdome, with krewe members tossing out beads, doubloons, cups, stuffed animals and MoonPies. This party (which included the rock band Chicago) went on into the wee hours of the morning, when a mile-long line of taxis waited to take partygoers back to their hotels.

But I still had one more Mardi Gras experience I needed to fulfill—to throw beads myself. So the next year I joined the Mystic Krewe of Barkus on behalf of my dog, Gypsy. And in 2005, she had the honor of walking in the Barkus parade. I held her leash and threw strands of beads that featured bones and a medallion that said "Wassup Dog!" The crowd loved them.

The magic of Mardi Gras endures the passage of time. And it was just like in the movies, only better.

Carol Anne Lake • Port Clinton, OH

HYPED UP
A Mardi Gras crowd reaches enthusiastically for trinkets during a New Orleans parade on Feb. 14, 1961.

Pictures from the Past

MARDI GRAS

QUEEN CARESSE

In 1969 my daughter Caresse was 18 years old. The Krewe of Noblads named her the queen of their Mardi Gras ball. (Noblads stands for the NOBles' LADies, a women's krewe sponsored by the Shriners.)

Beverly DeGeorge • Covington, LA

BE A CLOWN

As descendants of a long proud line of New Orleanians, we wanted to make sure our children took part in Mardi Gras fun. In 1972, the Conaway kids dressed as clowns, wearing pompom-decorated costumes made by my husband Ron's mother, Mathilda Meyers Conaway. Clockwise from top left, the jesters are Ron Jr., 8; Mark, 6; Darrin, 2; and Michael, 4.

Linda Conaway

VACATION VIEW

Dripping with parade beads, my husband, Robert, and I stand in front of steamboats from the 19th century that tour the Mississippi riverfront. We were in New Orleans for Mardi Gras 2008. The food was great! We had king cake for breakfast and the best shrimp we had ever eaten.

Carolyn Jackson

LITTLE LADY

Mardi Gras is a big part of our Louisiana history. We wore costumes every year. This is our daughter Caresse around 1960.

Beverly DeGeorge
Covington, LA

BON TEMPS

Crowds fill downtown New Orleans for a Mardi Gras parade in the 1950s. This is one photo of several that my husband, Bill, took during a trip to the Crescent City.

Ann Stear • *Rochester, NY*

(More of Bill's vacation photos can be seen on pages 36 and 37.)

Storm Before the Calm

New Orleans' Mardi Gras is a fabulous last splash before the Lenten fast.

3

BIG EASY FUN

From New Orleans' birth in 1718, Mardi Gras grew steadily grander and more ornate, according to the site *mardigrasneworleans.com*. In the early 1740s, Louisiana's governor, the Marquis de Vaudreuil, set up society balls. By the 1830s, there were street processions. Floats, or "tableaux cars," were common by the 1850s, and the King of Carnival, Rex, was introduced in 1872.

When Bill Stear attended Mardi Gras in the 1950s, it was the roiling carnival we know and love today. He captured the pageantry in these pictures, donated by his wife, Ann, of Rochester, New York.

1, 4: *Colorful floats with merry krewes.*
2: *A Groucho Marx mask and Victorian garb—anything goes!*
3, 5: *Dressing up is a time-honored tradition for Fat Tuesday celebrations.*

"I Wish You Luck"

On St. Patrick's Day, friends and family often sent blessings to each other via postcards. May these vintage cards bring you not only a smile, but also the best of luck.

The Wearing of the Green

St. Patrick's Day

"The best of luck will always wait upon you
If you pick up on the road a horse's shoe."

The Top o' the Mornin to you

SMILES ACROSS THE MILES

With a little luck of the Irish, they plant the seeds of gardening love in their grandchildren.

My wife, Carole, and I love to grow dahlias. Our acreage has many places for us to showcase these carefree, adaptable flowers.

Dahlias flourish in beds, borders and containers. Varying in height and width, they bloom with vibrant hues nonstop from July to frost. Honeybees and butterflies visit them.

Every October, after a cool, sunny stretch of weather, we collect seeds from our favorite dahlia plants.

"Jennie will love this color," Carole says, as she plucks a dried seed head from a wine-colored Figaro dahlia for our daughter.

Jennie's kids, Miles and Lara, are at the age when they're fascinated by watching new life take root. Our son Jimmy's kids, Nathan and Noelle, are a little younger, but they're just as eager to sow special seeds from Grandma and Grandpa's gardens.

After plucking one of the dried seedpods, I gently rub it between my fingers, releasing the seeds into a labeled envelope.

We also tag special or sentimental plants whose tubers we'll be lifting after a killing frost. One gold-and-red beauty whose petals resemble a tropical sunset was given to Carole by a dear friend who passed away. It's always on her must-save list.

New Jersey winters are cold, snowy and long. But by mid-March, small birds warble at dawn, heralding longer and warmer days ahead. Our thoughts turn back to planting flowers and sharing the seeds we collected in fall.

"The grandkids are just going to love these," Carole predicts, as she looks at the smiling leprechauns, Kelly green shamrocks and verses about the luck of the Irish on the cards I'd picked out. In each one she inserts a little glassine envelope containing dahlia seeds chosen especially for that family member.

"Happy St. Patrick's Day, happy spring and happy planting," she writes. "Love, Grandma and Grandpa Flynn."

Timed just right, and with a bit of luck, our mailed cards will arrive on March 17.

George Flynn • Newton, New Jersey

From the Ould Sod

St. Patrick's Day Greeting

Oh! steer my bark
To Erin Isle
For Erin is my home

"A good friend is like a four-leaf clover:
hard to find and lucky to have."

Irish Proverb

The Joy of Easter and Spring

April Fools' jokes and giant chocolate eggs are sure to put smiles on kids' faces, and some adults', too!

In Betty's classroom, she was playing the pranks.

TEACHER'S TURN FOR TRICKS

An assignment that really got the kids thinking.

Instead of students pulling April Fools' pranks, I pulled one every five years on my sixth-grade class. We studied the United Nations in social studies, and with so many new countries joining, I gave an assignment to report on a "new" representative named Loo F. Lirpa. The man's name was April Fool spelled backward!

I told my students to watch TV, look at newspapers, use the library and ask their parents for help. The report was due April 1. They researched to the point that they frustrated the librarians. Sometimes a student guessed right, but most didn't. I taught in Pennsylvania for 40 years and loved it.

Betty Van Arsdale • Bel Air, MD

MOM'S 'JOKE' IS DELIVERED PERFECTLY

But Dad doesn't get the timing.

My friends Anna and Luke were expecting their first child in a few weeks. Anna was tidying in the kitchen when she called to Luke, who was reading the newspaper.

"I think it's time! Pull the car to the front curb while I get my bag."

Luke said, "OK, in a minute." He kept reading.

Anna was surprised. "Luke, we have to hurry. We have to drive to the hospital, because the baby is coming!"

"I want to finish this article about the Cincinnati Reds first," Luke said.

Anna couldn't believe her ears. For the past eight and a half months, he'd been just as excited about the baby as she was.

"What's the matter, Luke?" she asked. "Don't you understand? We have to get started—the drive will take about 30 minutes. Please get the car and I'll get my coat!"

Luke stayed where he was.

Bewildered by his behavior, Anna picked up the phone and called an ambulance. She gave the address and told them she was pregnant and had to get to the hospital.

When the ambulance arrived, Luke finally put down the paper and stood up.

"Why did you call an ambulance?" he asked. "That costs big bucks, and we both know you're playing a joke on me—the baby isn't due for two more weeks!"

Anna didn't answer because the emergency worker was helping her down the porch steps and into the ambulance. Luke stared in complete disbelief as the ambulance took off quickly with its siren blaring.

Later, Luke stood at the window of the hospital nursery as a nurse held up a small blanket-clad bundle for his inspection.

Showing the baby to the new father, the nurse said, "Come on, little Debbie. Meet your daddy, who just happens to be the biggest April fool of 1953!"

Helen Liskowiak • Urbana, OH

HOW DID SHE KNOW IT WAS HIM?

In 1947, I was a legendary high school sophomore prankster in a very small town. On a sunny spring day, as several of my buddies and I walked to school, we passed a wisteria bush full of white-headed bumblebees. We each caught one, tied a thread around the bee's thorax, and proudly marched to school with the bee flying ahead.

We got to the room and put our bees into our teacher's desk drawer. The whole class waited. She came in and opened the drawer, and the bees came flying out. She screamed and then yelled, "Housman!" How did she know it was me?

Jack Housman
Spring Grove, PA

The Six-Day Engagement

My boyfriend of three years returned from Navy boot camp, picked me up from college during Easter vacation and proposed to me on a Monday. On Wednesday, he received orders to report for duty the following week in Washington, D.C. My mother said that time was too short to have a traditional wedding, so we decided to get married in a simple ceremony on the Easter Sunday before he left.

My sister took charge. She believed we could still have the wedding I'd always dreamed of. On Friday we went to Omaha, Nebraska, for our license, because Iowa required a three-day waiting period. I bought my wedding dress and had the napkins printed while my sister ordered the cake and got a photographer lined up. Everyone had new clothes for Easter, which became "wedding clothes."

Easter Sunday was also April 1. The pastor gave Larry a chance to leave and April fool everyone! But we have been together for more than 60 years. We fooled them all!

Sarah Wallis Bryceson
Osage Beach, MO

A little girl sings through her smile on a Sunday in the '60s.

BABY NEEDS A NEW PAIR OF SHOES

Dressing up and sharing the day with family.

Holiday hand-me-downs were normal for me. But around Easter time when I was 8 years old, my mother announced that we were going to Parke Snow's department store for a new outfit. As I was the youngest in the family, this was the adventure of a lifetime.

Ma picked out a blue dotted swiss dress with a velveteen bodice and a sash that tied in the back. I also got new Mary Jane patent leather shoes. No more of the brown Oxfords I'd had all my life. A white straw hat with a blue grosgrain ribbon around the brim and a pansy tucked into the side finished off the outfit.

On Easter morning, I slowly got dressed and looked in the mirror. I felt like Shirley Temple before she went onstage. All of the family still living at home paraded to church together. After church, the siblings, spouses and children gathered at home. It was chaotic, with everyone chatting at the same time and bumping into one another. Pa was the chef du jour. Assignments were given for all the odds and ends the meal entailed. The tablecloth consisted of long sheets of white paper from the 4-foot-tall roll my father had brought home from the paper mill where he worked. When everyone finished eating, my older brothers told jokes and anecdotes. I can still hear the laughter after all these years.

Joyce T. Rollins • Derry, NH

Here I am in an adorable Easter moment from 1947, fluffy bunny and all!

William Sharpe

A Big Basket of Treats

Decades later, I can still tell you all the Easter egg hiding spots: behind the fancy lamp, inside the vase, on the window ledges, along each stair step, under the couch and, finally, always one in Dad's shoe!

Mary Fosnow

I remember Mom and Dad boiling a load of eggs—we had hens, so we always had eggs on hand. There were five of us girls, and we would see who could eat the most! Later on, we'd take a needle and poke a little hole in each end of our eggs, then blow them out and paint them. Oh, the memories!

Marilyn Matheson

Easter was always fun for gathering eggs. When I was 9 years old, I found a prizewinning egg and won a white bunny that I named Thumper. I walked Thumper on a dog leash, gave him chocolate chip cookies before feeding him his pellets, and even had him baptized at my church!

Kathy Richard

Pink was the power color for Rita's family at Easter.

THE EASTER BUNNY LEFT HIS MARK

When I was 5 years old, in 1965, my family lived on a small farm southwest of Madison, South Dakota. My mother was "Mrs. Clean," and everyone, including the Easter Bunny, wiped his or her feet before coming into the house.

The night before Easter, my folks dyed and hid the eggs. Then my mother took a clean white cotton dish towel and painted multicolored bunny tracks all over it with the leftover dye. She laid it in front of the door and painted more tracks up toward the doorknob. I was so excited when I woke up and saw where the bunny had wiped his feet—and with evidence like that, you just had to believe in the bunny!

Donna Owen • Madison, SD

The Pink Parade

I learned to sew as an 8-year-old 4-H Club girl in Utica, Nebraska. After I grew up and years went by, my family grew to include four daughters and one son. In 1965, I decided to create matching Easter clothes for all. Kathy, 15, and Marge, 13, both received three-piece suits—a jacket and a skirt in dusty rose and a shell top of blush pink. Luanne, 9, and Janet, 5, each wore a pink A-line dress with a rose jacket. And Bob sported a pink necktie and a pocket square to match. I sewed the final stitches at 2 a.m. on Easter. Now every Easter reminds me of our pink Easter parade.

Rita Cox • Chicago, IL

The Making of a Beautiful Holiday

My mother was one of the most creative people I've ever known. She could sew, cook, can foods from the garden and decorate the house for every season. Each year for Easter, Mom would take the Easter dresses, hats and headbands from the previous year and "make them new." She bought new flowers, ribbons and lace and stayed up late at night finishing her creations. I remember getting up on Easter morning to see our outfits all ready for us to put on and wear to church. We always felt so proud to wear what she had made for us. Dad would always smile and tell us how pretty we looked. And even our little brother, Jim, was sharply dressed! In the picture at right, we are sitting in the bay window of our home, overlooking the Mississippi River in Rice, Minnesota. We had found our hidden Easter baskets, and we were ready to go to church.

Kathleen R. Surma • *St. Cloud, MN*

From left: Karen, Kathleen, Jayne, Peggy and Jim with baskets of delicious goodies the Easter Bunny brought for them in 1959.

No kid could resist indulging in this Easter treat.

THE GIANT CHOCOLATE EGG

Even though my family of 15 children was poor growing up in Eureka, Kansas, we still greatly anticipated Easter. There were so many things to experience: the citywide Easter egg hunt that paid 10 cents for every egg we collected, the new dresses our mother made for us girls and the fun we had trying to outdo one another decorating eggs.

With all of that going on, it might be hard to believe there was something even more exciting: a special gift our oldest brother, Dwight, sent us each year. He lived in New Jersey and always found the most beautiful Easter eggs filled with coconut, covered in chocolate, and decorated with spring flowers (pictured). We rarely had sweets, so I'm sure we drove our mother crazy asking her to cut into one. It was so big that all of us, and a few neighborhood kids, had stomachaches for a week.

Barbara Bilson Lutt • *El Dorado, KS*

The stainless steel rooftop tiara merited a reference to royal headgear.

FIT FOR A QUEEN

His Easter car with its fancy tiara is a keeper.

Almost as far back as I can remember, I have loved the 1956 Ford Fairlane Crown Victoria's perfect lines and fancied owning one. Over the years, I've owned three, including the top-of-the-line version that I still have.

I bought the first one from my brother in 1987, fixed it up, used it for car shows and fun, then sold it for a $200 profit. In 1989, I bought my "keeper" and gradually brought it back to its current restored condition.

Several years later I bought a third one in Long Island, New York. It had only 20,000 miles on it, but required some restoration. I fixed it up, used it daily for a few years and then sold it to a friend who thought it was the nicest car in his large collection.

The version I still own was dubbed the Easter car because the stainless steel tiara across the roof gave it the appearance of an Easter basket with a handle. And the car's factory options for pastel colors—yellow, pink, green, blue and orange—put an exclamation point on the nickname.

Mine is from the Easter car's second year of production, when only about one-fourth as many cars were produced as in the introductory year. So the second-year model, with updates like heavier stainless and chrome and a larger engine, is more desirable to collectors.

It also had the new "lifeguard design" features—including the deep-dish steering wheel, padded dash and seat belt options. Many (including me) regard this as one of the most beautiful cars ever produced for the average driver. Back then it sold for about $2,400.

Today it's worth a little more, though I doubt I'll ever sell. My wife, Linda, and I have refined it through the years. In our eyes, it's still incredibly beautiful.

Ken Colbert • Mount Pleasant, PA

LOVE IN A PAPER BAG

Mom's Easter custom endures for generations.

When my mother, Catherine, spoke of grandchildren and customs, she always said: "Be careful what you start, because then you have to continue."

She was probably thinking about Easter bags.

It began the first Easter after the birth of my oldest son, her first grandchild. He was about 5 months old and way too young for an Easter basket full of jelly beans, chocolate and other sugary candies. Instead, she bought food, clothing, diapers and other items that we needed for the baby.

When she spread out all that booty on the floor, it wouldn't fit into one Easter basket. So she had to use a brown paper bag from the local supermarket.

But there was a problem. The bag didn't look anything like an Easter basket. Sure, it held many items, but it looked more like she'd just come back from grocery shopping. Where was the Easter theme?

She turned to my father for help because he could draw. He drew Easter characters on the bag, and they both filled them in with bright colors. Covered in decorations, the bag looked like an Easter basket.

This tradition continued through nine grandchildren. For almost 20 years after my father, Andrew, died, Mom made the bags herself. Each grandchild received one until the age of 12. Then, after 12, he or she usually got an Easter card with a little cash.

Those grandchildren now range in age from 12 to 40 years old, and some still have their last Easter bag. When my wife and I had our first grandchild in 2008, we revived the tradition. Now, we have six grandchildren, and Mom lived to meet all of them.

Truthfully, neither my wife nor I can draw, so we glue clip art we find online or window decals to the bags. We shop for what the kids like and for what the parents approve. The bags overflow with goodies, toys and books.

The biggest problem in this age of plastic bags is finding paper bags without any lettering on them. It takes time and patience, but we manage to do it.

Our grandchildren anticipate diving into their bags. They love them so much that we've started a similar tradition for Halloween.

As Mom said, we should have been careful what we started.

Andrew Ricchiuti • Sewell, NJ

EASTERS TO REMEMBER

*Spring flowers, colorful candy and sunrise services
made the occasion especially memorable.*

The Easters of my childhood were nothing like today. They were simple.

Growing up in the '50s, my sisters and I could always anticipate a visit from the Easter Bunny. As soon as holiday goodies arrived in all the stores uptown, our father went shopping.

I couldn't wait to rip the bags apart and dig out the black jelly beans—the best kind. I finally figured out that we had so many sweets because Dad loved candy, and that was fine with me. Since we didn't eat it every day, those treats were special.

On the spiritual side, though, the highlight of my Easters was those early sunrise services at Mount Pleasant CME Church in rural Hope, Arkansas. We got up long before daybreak, dressed in our best, piled into the car and headed off to church. I liked it when this holy day came in late April, as I preferred attending services on a warm, sunny morning when I didn't have to wear a sweater over my pretty dress.

The air would be pungent with the sweetness of early spring. Daffodils bloomed up and down the highway—a sure sign that spring had brought Easter along with it.

Like us, believers across the world would attend church before the break of dawn, in keeping with the spirit of Christ's resurrection, when Mary Magdalene and the other women went to the tomb before the rising of the sun. When we gather on Easter morning, we are those women. We are looking for him, too, as we commemorate the celebration of our risen Savior.

As the sun peeped into the windows at Mount Pleasant, the congregation began singing an old traditional Easter hymn, "He Arose." I never saw that composition in any songbook. It may have been made up by the old-timers in those not-so-modern country churches. But as we worshipped in glorious song, Jesus' resurrection became as real to me as though he arose that very morning.

Southern black women wear their finest to church anyway, but Easter was an extravaganza. I adored

Morning worship at country churches is the highlight of the Easter celebration.

those sweet-smelling ladies in their fancy hats, frilly dresses with full petticoats underneath and the highest heeled shoes they could walk in. Those sisters strutted down the aisle proudly, as though they were marching in the Easter parade—heads held high, heels clicking and pretty dresses flowing in the gentle breeze.

Besides the "fashion show" at church, Easter was not as festive as Christmas. But the brightly colored eggs and candy, a beautiful new dress, the Easter Bunny, spring's budding flowers and soft, green grass added beauty and simple joy to the occasion.

Wilma Williams • Los Angeles, CA

BUSY MOM'S GREATEST GIFT

She shared her talents with those less fortunate.

Mother never liked to sew. Even though she was good at it, she found it more of a chore than a pleasure. Still, she never complained as she made us everyday dresses for school, shorts for camp and Easter dresses for church.

Easter was an especially busy time around our house. Mom and Dad sang in the adult choir, and we kids sang in the youth choir. The days leading up to Easter were filled with practicing, shopping, cooking and sewing.

One Easter seemed particularly hectic, and I noticed Mom spending more time than usual at the sewing machine. A few days before the holiday, she asked me to run an errand with her. We drove to the Salvation Army, where she pulled two new dresses from the backseat. I realized that this was what she'd been working on for the past couple of weeks.

"My Sunday school class is making Easter dresses for needy kids," she explained. "The Salvation Army gave me the measurements, and two girls are supposed to be waiting here to try them on."

Inside, two little girls smiled shyly as they took their new dresses from Mom and went to try them on. A few minutes later, two beautiful young ladies appeared. They had been transformed. As the girls thanked us, Mother just smiled.

We never spoke of that Easter again, but I'll always remember how my mother gave her time to make dresses for two children in need. I knew her gift had been a true labor of love.

Cathy Myers • Bullard, TX

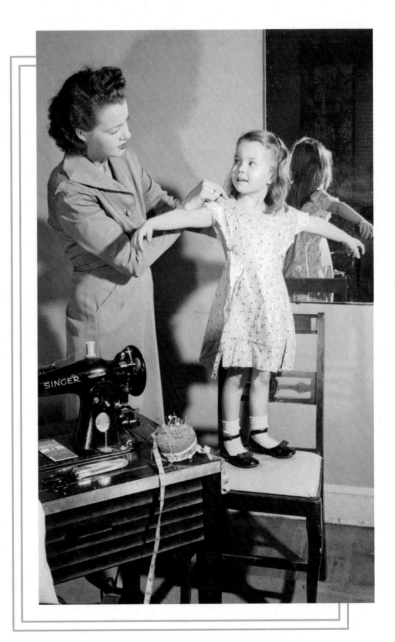

Moms sew love into every stitch.

SCRAMBLING FOR EGGS

An Easter fiasco sends the adults on the hunt.

One Easter weekend, my in-laws, John and Corky, planned a big egg hunt at my daughter's house.

They bought 96 plastic eggs and lots of candy to fill them. John and I would hide the eggs, and then my younger children and grandchildren would hunt for them.

"You think you can find some good hiding places?" John asked.

"I can find some great places to hide the eggs," I joked, "but with my memory, I'll never be able to find them all."

He laughed. "If there's candy in them, the children will find them."

The next morning, we were still asleep when the grandchildren pounced on us. "Is it time to hunt the Easter eggs, Grandpa?" my granddaughter asked.

I knew I wasn't going to get any more sleep, so I got up and cooked breakfast. Afterward, it was all we could do to keep the kids inside while John and I hid the eggs.

We worked hard to find the best spots, and it took about 20 minutes to hide them. We'd just finished and told the children they could hunt, when Corky appeared with a big bag of candy.

"John," she asked, "have you seen the plastic eggs that I bought? I can't find them."

John glanced at me and turned to Corky. "You didn't fill them?"

"No," she replied. "I was just getting ready to."

My grandson came over to show me a plastic egg he found. I opened it and, sure enough, it was empty. We collected the ones the children had found and shooed them back inside so that John and I could try to find the rest. When we finished, we could only find 82.

John grinned at me. "I guess you were right. We could hide our own Easter eggs and never find them."

Corky filled the ones we found, and John and I hid them again. We kept a bag of candy with us, and when the children found one of the empty rogue eggs, we magically filled it for them. But then they realized that if they emptied the full ones and brought them back to us, we'd fill those, too.

Pretty soon our bag was empty. We hadn't planned to give them all of the candy; it just worked out that way. My little granddaughter climbed on my lap and said, "Grandpa, I'm glad you're forgetful."

I smiled and hugged her. I guess every cloud has a silver lining.

Daris Howard • St. Anthony, ID

Easter Wishes

Charming cards depict treasures of springtime.

After mass production made greeting cards affordable for everyone in the late 19th century, sending them at holidays became something of a craze. Easter cards used sacred and secular symbols to mark spring's arrival—icons such as the cross honor the Christian observance, while budding apple trees, fat bunnies and hatchlings in the ever-present egg symbolize awakening. A quirky scene of chicks under a sprig of pussy willows has an unexpected tongue-in-cheep humor.

'Tis just a little
Easter card
That's come from
far away,
To let you know
A Friend of yours
Thought of you
today

Easter Greetings

EASTER GREETINGS

Pictures from the Past

EASTER

ALL DOLLED UP

Judy, Bonnie and I wore our Easter finery to visit the Children's Museum of Indianapolis in 1953. Dad's workplace, GM's Allison Division, sponsored the trip for employees' children.

Larry W. Gates • *Bargersville, IN*

COLD DAY FOR FUN

Our neighborhood held an Easter egg hunt at Fanny Duncan's farm in Floyd County in 1951. We had to bundle up because it was so cold, but we had a great time. I'm in the first row, far right.

Berchard Lee Hatcher
Stuart, VA

SUNDAY DRIVE

This photo of my big brother, Myron Frost, and me was taken on Easter Sunday of 1928 at our family farm outside of Burley, Idaho. I was 2½ years old and Myron was 4. We were going to our grandparents' house in town for Easter dinner. The car was our family's first, a Model T Ford bought in 1926. Myron joined the Navy at age 19 and was lost at sea serving his country in World War II.

Celia Frost Gilmour • Boise, ID

PATTERNED AFTER MOM

My mother, Wilma Hawes Connely, and I modeled the blue and white striped Easter dresses she made for us in 1962. I was 6.

Connie Connely • Tulsa, OK

EASTER BREAK

While visiting Great Smoky Mountains National Park in 1951, my sisters Barbara May and Patricia and I got a special treat when we had our picture taken with this giant rabbit topiary.

Ina Briggs • Elizabethton, TN

THE SPRING LOOK

In March 1949, myself (front row center) and fellow Girl Scouts (continuing clockwise: Marilyn Roberts, Carolyn Jones, Gwendolyn Knights, Donna Wheelock and Nancy Smith) were in a spring fashion show in Waterville, Maine. My aunt Gwendolyn Foster (in dress) sang "Easter Parade" and "Alice Blue Gown" as each bunny escorted a model down the runway.

Dyla Greenlaw • Yemassee, SC

A BEVY OF BEAUTIFUL BONNETS

Easter Sunday for the Hutchinson household in 1957 meant that my little girls sported new bonnets to church, while my 2½-year-old son showed off his fresh brimmed hat. Back row: Patsy, age 4; Myra, age 6; Louise, age 5. Front row: Mary Jean, 18 months; and Audrey, age 3.

Jane Hutchinson • Billings, MT

EASTER IN PANAMA

In 1962, my dad, Victor Robison, was stationed in Panama. On Easter morning, we posed for a picture taken by my mom, Margaret. Dad holds my sister Jenny. Mom tells me I was a real stinker that day.

Susan Nanette McKey
Colorado Springs, CO

EGGS APLENTY

Girl found fun by the cartonful every spring.

Excited for the start of an Easter egg hunt, little Linda smiles for Mom (below). She scrambles to uncover hidden holiday treats at a local park (left).

There's no such thing as too many Easter eggs. As a child in the late 1950s, I always looked forward to hunting for and coloring eggs, then seeing more on display at Eggshelland, a seasonal attraction near our home in Parma, Ohio.

Located in Lyndhurst, Eggshelland showcased the masterful work of Ron Manolio, who painted thousands of hollow eggs that he and his wife, Betty, used to create elaborate designs on their lawn each year. Families like mine flooded the Manolios' yard to marvel at their themed displays.

My Easter egg-stravaganza didn't end there. After leaving Eggshelland, Mom and I would head for an egg hunt in a local park, where several hundred children gathered at the starting line. When someone blew a whistle, we'd stampede across a field in search of the hidden treasures.

Kids crushed hundreds of eggs under their shoes, while excited hands mishandled many others, breaking the shells and spilling the yellow yolks. I'll never forget the time I returned to my mother, eggless and in tears. But she consoled me, reminding me that I still had a couple dozen eggs to color at home.

When Easter morning finally arrived, I discovered the best surprise of all: a basket loaded with eggs, chocolates and gifts delivered by my flop-eared friend, the Easter Bunny.

Linda Lehmann Masek • Northfield, OH

"In spring 1958, I was 14 months, sitting on the lap of a giant, scary-looking Easter Bunny. My sister, Carol, 3½, is smiling, apparently enjoying my distress."

Jane Christie Gibson • *Allentown, PA*

Independence Day and Parades Galore

Strike up the band and break out the red, white and blue as Americans commemorate Memorial Day and more.

LEADING THE MEMORIAL DAY PARADE

The patriotic excitement was contagious.

Uncle Sam will always be special to me. Our town was one of the most patriotic in our area, and the students in our school always marched in the annual Memorial Day parade. When I was 11 or 12, I was selected by our music director to play the part of Uncle Sam and lead our school. I never ran home so fast as that day, bursting with pride as I told Mom and Dad about my great honor.

On the morning of the parade, I refused to allow my dad to drive me; I preferred to walk all the way to school, thereby meeting many of our citizens heading for the parade and ceremonies. It was a thrill to hear them make positive remarks about my red, white and blue outfit and my tall stovepipe hat. I was simply overflowing with pride knowing that I was representing not only my school but also my town, state and country. That day instilled in me a great respect for our flag and nation that has remained with me throughout my life.

Francis Gros Louis • Leesburg, VA

MAJORETTES
READY TO MARCH

Memorial Day is about family and honoring the fallen.

My sisters Sharon, Doris and Betty, along with our Aunt Sue and I, were in the American Legion's majorette unit and marched in every holiday parade in Toledo, Ohio, in the early 1950s. There were 12 kids in my family—seven sisters, five brothers—but we were the majorettes.

Our uniforms were royal blue corduroy with gold roping, and we wore wrist cuffs, boots and hats that had inner cardboard liners. Our mother, Evelyn Clarke, and grandmother Gertrude Gross made the uniforms by hand.

Our favorite parade was on Memorial Day, when we marched to the cemetery along with several hundred friends and family watching. When we arrived at the cemetery, priests celebrated Mass in the open area and dedicated it to the fallen soldiers. At that time, even the kids knew the real meaning of Memorial Day and respected the ceremonies. After the ceremonies, it was time for picnics, fireworks and baseball at Joe E. Brown Park.

Remembrance, food, family and fun—there was no better way to celebrate Memorial Day than that.

Helen Price • Springfield, IL

Break time for twirlers, from left, Aunt Sue, Sharon, Helen, Doris and Betty.

Decoration Day

In 1956, my first year as a Boy Scout in West Homestead, Pennsylvania, I marched in my first parade, which commemorated Decoration Day, the forerunner to Memorial Day. The parade ended in a solemn gathering at a cemetery on a hilltop in Munhall, a company town outside of Pittsburgh.

Though World War II had ended 11 years earlier, it remained a painful memory for the people at the cemetery that day. Many had lost someone in the war. My friend Bobby sang "My Buddy," which is about the loss of a close friend. When he finished, the crowd stood silent. Many were sobbing—even the steelworkers had broken down in tears.

Growing up during those early postwar years meant learning about war in terms of heroism and patriotism. It took that Decoration Day parade and ceremony for me to fully understand war's true cost.

George Toth • Gaithersburg, MD

REMEMBERING THOSE NO LONGER WITH US

Marching in the annual Hackettstown, New Jersey, Memorial Day parade in 1960, I wore my Girl Scout uniform. My widowed mother, Mary, who was an American Legion Auxiliary member and a Gold Star Mother (her oldest son, my brother Larry, had died in Korea), dressed in white. My middle brother, Bill, the tall Boy Scout, and my youngest brother, Benny, a Cub Scout, are on the left. My older sister Peggy, on the right, marched beside our mother. My oldest sister, Judy, took this photo.

Cathy Foulk • Bloomsbury, NJ

SOLEMN OBSERVANCE
I took this photo on Memorial Day 1966 in Joliet, Illinois. The band played and the American flag waved in the breeze.

Bill Larson • *Batavia, IL*

IN TRIBUTE
Memorial Day parade marchers head down Main Street in Southington, Connecticut, in 1942. The town's war factories hadn't closed for the holiday, which accounts for the sparse crowd.

Campfire Collective

Almost everything I owned when I was 4 years old had once belonged to my older brother or sister. Imagine how special I felt when my grandmother made an outfit for me to wear while joining her on a float in the 1976 Sweet Valley Fireman's Memorial Day Parade. My grandparents lived in nearby Hunlock Creek, Pennsylvania, and were involved with the Sweet Valley Volunteer Fire Co. Many of the firefighters, along with my grandparents, parents, aunts and uncles, belonged to the Good Sam Club, and we traveled in RVs together every weekend to visit campgrounds around northeastern Pennsylvania. Sitting around a campfire with friends and relatives was a nice way to grow up.

Dawn Kaplanski • Dallas, PA

The parade float that Dawn and her grandmother sat on was a flatbed trailer with a campfire depicting settlers of 1776. They were towed by a new motor home to represent camping's evolution.

ONE OF THE SCOUTS

My husband, Bill, marching at far left, was 7 when he participated with other Boy Scouts in this Memorial Day parade. It took place in Cumberland, Rhode Island, in 1948.

Joanne O'Neill Kane • Johnston, RI

Rex the Horse

Osage County, Oklahoma, was worn thin in 1936. Neighbors kept up with one another by watching the clotheslines—khaki shirts meant someone had work; white shirts meant they were still looking. My father, Dwight, had an oil company job.

With careful saving and a loan from my grandmother, my parents bought a 10-acre farm along the Arkansas River. After work and on weekends, Dad trained horses, so there were always new animals in the big barn. But when a neighbor was forced to give up his farm, he tearfully gave us his three horses, including a magnificent Morgan named Rex. He wasn't easy to handle, and he became Dad's.

As the Depression began to recede, nearby Ponca City geared up for the return of the Fourth of July parade in 1939, after a four-year absence. My dad—on Rex, the handsomest horse in the county—was chosen to lead the parade. Rex pranced, walked sideways and was generally obnoxious—but he was the star of the parade.

David Tarpenning • Oklahoma City, OK

THANKS, MOM AND DAD

The summer I was 16, a friend asked me to ride on a float in the Fourth of July parade. I wouldn't have to do anything but smile and wave to the crowd—in my swimsuit. I didn't think my parents would approve, and they didn't, so I reluctantly told my friend no.

I still wanted to see the parade and get a look at that float, so I joined the crowd lining the street. Finally, it rolled by, festooned with red, white and blue crepe paper. It took my breath away—because it was a big dump truck! My friend was not riding on the so-called "float." No one was on it but the driver.

Boy, was I relieved.

Maryellen Coombs
Racine, WI

Dwight trained horses at the family's new farm. Here he is on Rex, leading Ponca City's Fourth of July parade in 1939.

Crowds packed the Independence Mall area of Philadelphia, Pennsylvania—including the Liberty Bell Pavilion (in the foreground) for a parade on July 4, 1976.

GOTTA LOVE A PARADE

Drumbeats echoed as freedom rang.

Despite seeing only the tops of tubas, flagpoles, tricorn hats and President Gerald Ford's head, I have the best red, white and blue memories of being in the very place where the first Fourth of July happened 200 years earlier.

As a native Philadelphian and a newly minted member of Friends of Independence National Historical Park, the first chartered Friends group in the National Park Service, I was eager to staff the table across the street from Independence Square, where I promoted Friends membership and activities. However, at 5 feet 1 inch, I had a hard time seeing over the taller members of the crowd.

But what a moment to be present for. President Ford's speech was deliberate but moving. The music stirred and flags inspired as the five-hour parade streamed by and floats from every state captured our imaginations. Most of all, the feeling of pride in our country was palpable.

It was an honor to be there and feel the patriotism that our country's founders, both men and women, had inspired in 1776.

Linda Abby Fein • *Philadelphia, PA*

Coming Together

Celebrate the Fourth with a float, a parade and... a snowball fight?

Out here at the remote Cottonwood Ranch in northeastern Nevada, cowboys, guests, friends and neighbors celebrate the Fourth of July with hearts as big as the vast blue skies and with patriotism as steadfast and unshakable as the mighty Jarbidge Mountains.

Considering the nearest paved road is 30 miles away and the closest town of Wells is a distant 70 miles, a ranch owner named Irene "Renie" Smith and her late husband, Horace, launched a genuine star-spangled tradition in 2005.

They started an hour-long parade and patriotic program at their fifth-generation cattle, horse and guest ranch in the scenic O'Neil Basin.

"Our only rule is no one is a bystander. Everyone has to join in and participate somehow," says Renie, 86, who estimates that between 20 and 80 people have been in the parade. "We make floats with whatever material is around and drive our trucks, tractors, wagons and four-wheelers or ride our horses."

The other unwritten rule is that everyone casts aside their political differences for the day. "We're all Americans," Renie says. "It does not matter what your politics are. We live in a wonderful country with freedom and liberty."

In the morning, everyone begins decorating their four-wheelers, floats and four-legged companions. At about 4 p.m. participants start to get fired up for the festivities.

Renie leads the parade as grand marshal, riding in an all-terrain vehicle along a sagebrush-lined route from the ranch's lodge to a meadow. She flies a flag presented to the family during a military

1

3

funeral for her father-in-law, Emery, a World War I veteran.

In the meadow, the patriots say the Pledge of Allegiance and salute all veterans, "especially those in our own family and crew," says Alecia Maxey, who along with her husband, Tom, is a partner in the ranch's cattle business.

The Smiths' son Agee followed his grandfather's and father's footsteps and served during the Vietnam War. In the Maxey family, Tom's dad served in Germany at the end of World War II. "Tom and I both have uncles who are veterans," Alecia says. "And our godson graduated from West Point."

With the veterans in mind, the celebrants sing "The Star-Spangled Banner," "Home Means Nevada," "God Bless America" and "America the Beautiful."

Summing up the ceremony, Alecia says, "Whenever we come together as Americans celebrating freedom, we have a strong sense of camaraderie that envelops us. We think of our founding fathers' vision and struggles, and we remember all the people who have sacrificed so that we can celebrate and live in this great country."

After the tribute ends, cowboy humor kicks in. Giggles and squeals erupt as a water-truck driver sprays everyone. Some years, a snowball fight has broken out—courtesy of cowboys who filled up picnic coolers with the frosty remnants of winter they scooped up from the nearby mountains.

With the fifth generation of Smiths helping to run the ranch, Renie says, "They'll make sure our parade continues to be a tradition for all of us."

Dianna Troyer • Pocatello, ID

1: *The annual parade begins at the ranch gate.*
2: *Participants sing and celebrate America.*
3: *Cowboys cheer in a boisterous hats-off salute to freedom.*
4: *Uncle Sam waves from atop a four-wheeler, with Lady Liberty close behind.*

PATRIOTISM ON PARADE

When the whole family joins the fun, this includes the car.

John celebrates America's birthday by taking the grandkids for a ride in his restored Model T.

Every year my dad, John Arie of Bondville, Illinois, drives his 1911 Model T in the Fourth of July parade in the farming community of Seymour. It's always a really enjoyable event, with a great collection of old cars and tractors to admire. My brother Tim always rides with my dad to throw out candy.

The Fourth of July is Dad's favorite holiday, and he loves his car. He has had the Model T for more than 20 years. He had always wanted to own one, and when he finally found one to purchase, it was red and yellow! After completing its restoration,

he takes a lot of pride in it. In many ways the Model T is part of the family.

It's really important to Dad to have all of the grandkids with him in the parade. We have a big family, so the kids ride behind him on a decorated float.

Stacy Arie • *Champaign, Illinois*

FINANCIAL SECURITY

*Saving for the
American dream.*

THE RELAXED APPROACH

As this ad says, "You can really enjoy celebrating the 4th of July when your independence includes financial peace of mind"—just like this spectacled man who somehow is keeping his book dry in a swimming pool.

'61

BELIEF IN OPPORTUNITY

Working hard for one's money in America is just part of the plan, according to this *Reader's Digest* ad promoting federal Insured Savings and Loan Associations.

'62

Pictures from the Past

FOURTH OF JULY

YOUNG AND OLD

I love this picture of my grandsons Jonathon and Calvin closely watching the 2016 Fourth of July parade in Tamworth Village, New Hampshire.

Cheryl Alander • Bartlett, NH

LIGHTING UP THE NIGHT

A father and son proudly show their love of country as brilliant fireworks burst in the sky during a Fourth of July celebration.

Jack Tinney

TIME FOR FUN

This adorable picture includes myself (second from left) at age 4, with my cousins Albert, 2, and Floss, 5, and brothers Morrie, 6, and Leroy, 5, ringing in the Fourth of July in 1940 in patriotic style at our grandmom's house in New Jersey.

Patricia Waldron • *Joppa, MD*

PRIDE IN COUNTRY

I was lucky to grow up in White Lake, a village in northern Wisconsin. I remember how exciting it was to decorate my bike with streamers, flags and noisemakers for the Fourth of July parade. These two photos were taken in 1970. It seemed as if every kid in town was riding, pushing or pulling a red, white and blue bike, wagon or stroller. There were bands, floats and so many veterans—it was the first time most of us knew what it meant to feel patriotic.

Jane Whitt • *Stevens Point, WI*

RANK AND FILE

The United States celebrated its bicentennial throughout the year in 1976. On July 4, millions lined the streets of downtown Philadelphia, Pennsylvania, as a parade including Colonial soldier re-enactors marched past Independence Hall, where 200 years earlier the Declaration of Independence had been signed.

HUMAN FLAG

These young women in Crete, Nebraska, did quite a bit of extra sewing in 1923 to create this living tribute to Old Glory. I was one of the "stripe girls" (second from the right).

Bernice Sanderson • Los Angeles, CA

MOVABLE FEAST

My aunts and uncles lived very near each other in Monroeville, Pennsylvania, and Aunt Helen's front yard was the spot for many holiday gatherings. This picnic in 1951 included four generations of Bartleys. Aunt Helen is at far right.

Katrina Syska
East Pittsburgh, PA

READY FOR TAKEOFF

My sons Brad (left) and Bill loved to decorate their bikes for the Fourth of July parade in Sharonville, Ohio. We'd have a family conference on what best represented the occasion. In 1969, it was the evolution of flight, as America was about to put men on the moon.

Elizabeth Lamb • Albany, OR

A Grand Day Out

*Presidential parade passenger
makes for a lasting memory.*

In October 1909, my mother, Geneva Maze—a 15-year-old schoolgirl—stood patiently on a San Francisco street to see President William Howard Taft in a parade in his honor. The president likely was a memorable sight, but Geneva was more impressed by the man driving Taft's carriage. It was her father, Emile Maze.

Emile, a carriage driver since 1890, worked for an elite livery stable company that catered to the wealthy of San Francisco. Clients expected perfection. Once a woman complained that her driver had only one button instead of two on the back of his coat. She demanded he be replaced. Grandfather Emile had lost the button en route to the client's house and had no choice but to return to the stables to have a new button sewn on.

All drivers had a black silk top hat and three long coats, each corresponding to the color of the vehicle they were driving. They followed a stiff etiquette. Drivers did not help riders into the carriage but kept their eyes gazing forward, awaiting instructions. And they were not to look at the passengers but to focus on the tails of the horses.

Likely his nearly 20 years of experience made my grandfather the best choice to drive President Taft in 1909. On the day of the parade, he polished the maroon landau and groomed the two geldings, coincidentally named Taft and Sherman, and then donned his maroon coat.

He kept his eyes on the horses while his passengers boarded. They included Edward R. Taylor, mayor of San Francisco; James Gillett, governor of California; and

Archibald Butt, the presidential aide who later died on the Titanic. When the landau sagged heavily to one side, Emile knew that the hefty Taft had taken his seat. The carriage took a grand tour, winding along the city streets. The president was pleased to see all of the rebuilding since the earthquake of 1906.

At the end of the parade, in front of the St. Francis Hotel, Emile looked at his passengers for the first time. With a kindly smile, Taft put out his hand and Emile shook it. Then the president said something to his aide, who handed my grandfather a $50 bill—an enormous tip for someone who earned $2.50 a day.

Grandfather Emile often spoke of his day of glory and wondered if other presidents would have been so generous. He'd joke that Calvin Coolidge probably would have charged him $50 to shake his hand.

Wilma Hofheins • Mapleton, UT

2

1: *Carriage drivers for the Kelly Brothers, a livery stable company in San Francisco, pose for a group picture. In 1909 Wilma's grandfather worked for the stable.*

2: *President Taft doffs his hat during a 1909 parade through the streets of San Francisco. Emile, his driver, takes a rare glance away from his horses to smile for the camera.*

3: *Carriage driver Emile Maze sits ready by the stables before heading out on a job.*

1

3

THE RIDE OF HER LIFE

In 1959, I was in sixth grade in Lexington, Massachusetts. My neighbor let me ride his horse in a parade through downtown on Patriot's Day, which celebrates the first battle against the British in the American Revolution.

The kids who owned horses decorated them with red, white and blue crepe paper. My ride was a former racehorse and very high-strung. She was not happy with the crepe paper on her and the other horses. It made her nervous.

We inched along the route in front of the engines from the local fire stations. Suddenly the sirens sounded, and my horse bolted. She galloped the 2 miles right home to the barn, with me hanging on for dear life. We left a trail of red, white and blue crepe paper that I was picking out of the bushes and grass for many months afterward.

Suzy Hopkins • Denver, CO

Cool as a Camel

In 1966, I was 27 and the manager of the Firestone store in Merced, California. As a member of a Masonic lodge, I decided to join the Tehran Shrine in Fresno. The Shriners were going to have a ceremonial initiation and parade through downtown, with about 50 new-member candidates—plus three camels. They needed three men to lead the camels and three to ride them.

I quickly put my hand up, thinking, *How often do you get the chance to ride a camel?* They dressed me in Middle Eastern garb and helped me onto the camel. About halfway through the parade, my camel began to jump and buck. I let go and landed in the street on my feet.

A few days later, while driving the company truck, my chest began to hurt badly, so I was taken to the hospital with a possible heart attack. The Firestone home office in Los Angeles was notified that I'd had a heart attack on the job. An X-ray revealed a different ailment, however: When I had hit the ground, I'd jarred my chest muscles loose from my rib cage. So word quickly went back to the head office: "No heart attack; fell off of camel in parade."

For years friends sent me pictures of camels and camel figurines to remind me of my dubious parade ride.

Dick Johnson • Tulare, CA

PONY POWER

The summer of 1949, my late father, Lyle Herrington (first rider on the left), engineered a "chuck wagon" for the Calgary Stampede parade in Calgary, Alberta. Four Massey-Harris Pony tractors were the "horses," led by the wagon drivers. Four outriders on Pony tractors flanked the horses, just as it's done in a real chuck wagon race. The float received the award in the industrial section.

Audrey Herrington • Madoc, ON

Pictures from the Past

HOORAY FOR A PARADE

RALLY ROUND THE FLAGS

Boy Scouts parade at a soapbox derby in Richland, Washington, in 1959. Photo by Oran Bethel, Kennewick.

Alice Shea • *Kennewick, WA*

NATIONAL PARADE

It was very cold in Washington, D.C., the day of Nixon's second inauguration in 1973. I'm holding the flag over my parents, brother and sister. We look like we just arrived in America as immigrants from Russia.

Michael Wells • *Carlisle, PA*

LITTLE PIONEER

Loyalty Day parades held on May 1, were popular in the U.S. in the mid-'50s. I took this picture of a small "pioneer" with his miniature wagon in Burlington, Wisconsin.

Bruce Thompson • Waukesha, WI

RE-ENACTMENT TRIO

In July 1976, Bill Jones, John Ferguson and I marched around Philadelphia for the bicentennial.

Linda Formelio • Magnolia, DE

HERE THEY COME!

The Massachusetts State Guard was on parade in Athol in 1943. I'm an old-car buff, and I believe the '36 Plymouth in front of the lamppost is one I later acquired and still own.

Paul Robichaud • Orange, MA

A GIRL AND HER PONY

*Buck wasn't the palomino she had always wished for,
but she loved him anyway.*

For as long as I can remember, I have loved horses. Growing up, I dreamed of owning my very own. In my mind's eye, I saw myself sitting high in the saddle on a beautiful, well-bred palomino and riding in a parade.

I was so sure I would get a horse for my high school graduation gift. The whole school year, I talked about it. I often asked my mother, "What kind of horse are you getting me?" She'd just smile and shake her head.

On a warm day in May 1963, I looked out my bedroom window and saw a big Lane furniture truck pull up to our farmhouse, and I knew I had to forget about a horse and settle for a hope chest. Thank goodness for my wise mother; I was leaving home soon to start college—what would I have done with a horse? Still, the desire to own a horse never left me.

On another warm day many years later, my dream finally came true in the most unexpected way. Through the kindness of a scruffy-looking gentleman, I was blessed with an old stocky buckskin horse named...Buck. Yes, he was ugly and often temperamental, but he was a horse! Best of all, he warmed up to me, and I loved him.

One of the most memorable times I shared with old Buck was the day I got to ride him—with my husband, Ronald, by my side—in the Horse and Wagon parade hosted in our small town.

Early that morning, I brushed Buck until I thought my arms were going to fall off, trying to make him look somewhat presentable, but it was hopeless. Still, nothing was going to stop me from riding him in that parade.

Sporting my new cowgirl hat, gaucho pants and burgundy boots, I sat proudly in the saddle. As I waited for the parade to start, my heart raced. I could hardly contain my excitement.

Finally the moment came! Wagon wheels began to roll and horseshoes began to clop on the pavement.

And then it started to rain—not just a drizzle, but a heavy downpour. Ronald grinned at me from his own horse and asked, "Do you want to call it quits?"

*Joyce and Buck wait for
the parade to start.*

"No way," I replied, rain dripping from the brim of my brand-new hat, "I've waited a long time for this day!"

By the time the parade ended, my prized cowgirl outfit was drenched and my boots were filled with water. How funny I must have looked! Our kids got a good laugh at our pathetic rain-soaked condition.

Poor Buck looked more pitiful than ever—a far cry from a beautiful palomino. But I was so happy. My lifelong dream of riding in a parade had come true at last.

Joyce Noel Wyatt • Kodak, TN

"My daughter Mindy Sue and son David McKinley stand outside
our home in Grants in 1959. They had dressed up
to go to a rodeo parade that day."

David Button • Roswell, NM

A Haunting Halloween

Kids can't wait to get dressed up for free candy!
The costumes are certainly worth a laugh or a scare.

All Hallowed Sweets

Most candy brands go back to well before the 1950s, when giving out packaged treats at Halloween took hold. In the years since, these favorites have brightened the last night of October for millions of kids.

By Linda Kast

CANDY CORN

While working at Philadelphia-based Wunderle Candy Co. in the late 19th century, candymaker George Renninger invented a way to layer buttercream. The process produced a tricolored kernel-shaped candy that some called "chicken feed." By the 1950s, the renamed candy corn was synonymous with fall and especially Halloween. And what's the right way to eat candy corn? About 17% start with the yellow bottom, 31% start with the white top and 52% eat the whole piece at once.

100 GRAND

Named after a popular game show's ultimate prize, the Nestlé $100,000 bar was patented in 1964 before undergoing a name change in the 1980s to 100 Grand bar. The unusual flavor and texture combination of chocolate, caramel and crispy rice makes it a standout.

HERSHEY'S KISSES

The little chocolate bites were a market hit in 1907. One story has them named for the sound of the chocolate plopping onto the conveyor belt during production. The tissue-paper plume, as it's called, was trademarked in 1924. Silver was the sole color of aluminum foil used to wrap them until 1962, when Hershey introduced seasonal red and green wrappers. Today, more than 70 million flat-bottomed chocolate Kisses roll off the line daily in Hershey, Pennsylvania.

TOOTSIE ROLL

Leo Hirschfield, a candymaker who emigrated from Austria, introduced the Tootsie Roll to American consumers in 1905 as the first individually wrapped penny candy. He named the chewy delight after his daughter, Clara, nicknamed Tootsie. As inexpensive chocolate-flavored snacks that didn't melt, Tootsie Rolls sold well during the Depression. A military contract at the start of World War II turned them into GI favorites.

Dori Sonenschein, 6, bites into a Tootsie Roll on a New York street in 1961.

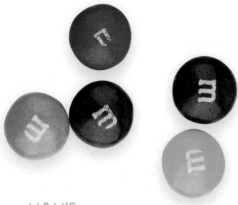

M&M'S

In Spain, during the country's civil war in the 1930s, Frank Mars' son Forrest saw soldiers eating chocolate morsels coated in hard candy that kept the bits from melting.

Forrest Mars patented his own formula and, in 1941, introduced the now-legendary morsels named for himself and his business partner in the venture, chocolate supplier Bruce Murrie, son of Hershey president William F.R. Murrie.

During WWII, under exclusive contract to the U.S. military, the candy was packaged in cardboard tubes.

This $1 billion brand was the first candy to go interstellar when the space shuttle launched in 1981 with M&M's aboard.

BABY RUTH

Babe Ruth probably did inspire the name of this popular candy bar, which came out in 1921—the same year the slugger wowed the country by hitting 59 home runs. But Otto Schnering of the Curtiss Candy Co. in Chicago would never admit it. Instead, Schnering claimed that he named the candy after President Grover Cleveland's daughter Ruth who died of diphtheria in 1904.

When Babe Ruth later endorsed a different bar named after him, Schnering sued to keep the new candy out of stores—and a patent judge upheld the claim.

In a twist-of-the-knife marketing ploy, Schnering later erected a billboard for Baby Ruth bars outside Chicago's Wrigley Field, where the Great Bambino is said to have called his shot before slamming a homer to center field during the 1932 World Series.

Two Ruths, Ruth Cleveland and the Babe, battle for naming rights to the candy bar.

SMARTIES

Edward Dee immigrated from England in 1949 and began making the sweet-and-sour discs in a New Jersey factory. Originally pressed using a repurposed WWII pellet-maker, the candies are called Rockets in Canada. Factories in New Jersey and Ontario run 24/7 producing the treats by the billions each year.

Edward coined the name Smarties to encourage kids to be smart and pursue education, according to his granddaughter and co-president Liz Dee.

MARY JANE

Boston candymaker Charles H. Miller Co. introduced Mary Janes, a taffy candy made of peanut butter and molasses, in 1914, and it quickly became a popular penny candy. More than a century later, Atkinson Candy Co. in Texas makes Mary Janes with a recipe and packaging—distinctive yellow and red waxed paper and an illustrated girl—virtually unchanged from the beginning. Original Mary Janes are rectangles. Round versions in orange and black wrappers known as Mary Jane Peanut Butter Kisses are Halloween staples.

OH HENRY!

Theories abound as to the origins of this chocolate, nut and nougat bar, but the strongest evidence supports its being invented by George Williamson in his Chicago candy shop around 1920. Corporate lore has the name coming from the shopgirls summoning a handsome young patron named Henry to help them with various tasks—"Oh Henry!"

LIFE SAVERS

Life savers launched in 1912 in one flavor, Pep-O-Mint, as a cool summer treat. Seven years later, six new flavors—Wint-O-Green, Cl-O-ve, Lic-O-Rice, Cinn-O-Mon, Vi-O-Let and Choc-O-Late—joined the product line in distinctive hand-wrapped foil packages. In 1935, the classic five flavors of pineapple, orange, lime, cherry and lemon were on a roll; they're still going strong.

CHOCOLATE FOR THE TROOPS

You can credit Americans returning from World War I with turning chocolate into a national craving. After seeing British soldiers with tins of King George Chocolates during the Great War, the U.S. Army Quartermaster Corps had to rethink its rations. It turned to chocolate as both an energy source and a morale perk, and solicited donations of 20-pound blocks from confectioners back home. The large blocks were cut to size, hand-wrapped and doled out to the troops. Those doughboys came home with an insatiable appetite for the sweet stuff.

The timing coincided with the passage of Prohibition (1920–'33), and chocolate became a substitute for alcohol's mood-boosting properties.

At the onset of WWII, combat rations for soldiers already had been part of an ongoing experiment started in 1937 between Hershey and the Army's quartermaster general. The final formula for the Field Ration D bar was a 4-ounce, 600-calorie chocolate food product that could withstand heat and keep a hungry GI alive. It's estimated that during the war

more than 3 billion bars shipped out to military personnel around the world.

During Operation Desert Storm in 1991, about 144,000 Hershey's Desert Bars, a chocolate bar that turned fudgy instead of liquid at high temperatures, went to the Middle East in soldiers' rations. Gen. H. Norman Schwarzkopf's troops gave them a thumbs-up, but Hershey discontinued the candy bar shortly after Desert Storm ended.

WHATCHAMACALLIT

Grasping for a perfect name, Hershey came out in 1978 with the Whatchamacallit, a chocolate-coated peanut-crisp-and-caramel candy bar.

In 2009, the Thingamajig, a chocolate-covered peanut-butter bar layered with cocoa crisps, launched as a limited-edition counterpart, only to disappear three years later.

The Whoozeewhatzit, boasting a crowdsourced name and similar ingredients to the other two, appeared in early 2021.

JOLLY RANCHER

The Jolly Rancher Co. was founded in Denver, Colorado, in 1949, and sold a variety of sweets. But owners Bill and Dorothy Harmsen eventually switched exclusively to hard candies.

Today's Jolly Ranchers come in apple, cherry, grape, watermelon and blue raspberry.

PIXY STIX

In 1942, Menlo Smith's father packaged and sold a powdered drink mix with sugar. With rationing keeping sugar and candy in short supply during WWII, kids bought penny packets of the sweet mix and used their fingers to eat it directly out of the package.

When Menlo Smith launched his candy company in St. Louis 10 years later, he rebranded the sugary powder as Lik-M-Aid. Sales topped $1 million in three years, but grocery stores stocked the drink mix only in summer. So in 1959, Smith repackaged it in straws and called it Pixy Stix.

From that original formula, Smith went on to create Nerds, Spree, SweeTarts and other Halloween-friendly confections.

'54

CURTIS CANDY

Americans purchase an estimated 160 million pounds of Halloween candy every year; the average treat haul each Oct. 31 per child can reach up to 7,000 calories.

SNICKERS

Candy mogul Frank Mars created the Snickers bar, named after his favorite racehorse, in 1930. Today, Snickers is a $2 billion brand. The confection's phenomenal worldwide popularity is likely due to a combination of mouth-pleasing tastes and textures—chocolate, caramel, peanuts and nougat—and an enduring marketing campaign that touts Snickers as the ultimate means to satisfy hunger cravings.

Halloween buddies John and Christine in 1970.

HIGHWAY ROBBERY

Halloween loot was in the bag, then calamity struck.

My fondest Halloween memory, strangely enough, is the result of a mean prank. I was trick-or-treating with my next-door neighbor, my first and lifelong friend, John Mazur. I don't remember what we were dressed as, but I'm certain we put a lot of time into making our costumes. Nor do I remember the weather, even though we'd surely hoped for weeks that it would be perfect. I don't even recall exactly how old we were—perhaps 9 or 10, since it was around 1972. But I do remember that it had been a hard night's work, and we were almost done making our rounds.

Our route had many three-family houses, and we'd diligently climbed the flights of steps to the back doors of numerous apartments to collect our loot. Then it happened: A group of pranksters, noticing our heavy bags, grabbed mine. We had a brief tug of war, which I lost, and my bag of treasure disappeared into the night, leaving me clutching a torn handle.

Not wanting our Halloween to be ruined, I got another bag and we went on. When we met up with our big brothers, they made a brotherly promise to get my candy back, but it was to no avail.

Our route ended at John's house, and I sadly dragged myself inside. We poured our candy onto the large wood table, but I could barely look at my little pile. What a haul John had! Full-size Butterfingers and 3 Musketeers, Marathons and Mounds, Smarties and wax lips—enough sugar to make a kid believe she'd caught a glimpse of heaven.

John pushed his mountain of goodies to one end of the table. Then he started: "One for you, one for me…" He gave up half his candy—the sweetest thing anyone ever did for me.

John lives across the country now, and we continue our friendship. But I really miss having him next door.

Christine Kidder • *Granby, CT*

TREATS OF THE PAST

Papier-mache lanterns were sold at five-and-dimes in the weeks leading up to Halloween.

Vintage lanterns shed light on holidays of old.

When I was in my 20s, a friend who was an antiques dealer had two Halloween-themed papier-mache lanterns in his shop. I couldn't stop admiring them. A week later, they came in the mail, safely packed with a note: "Enjoy." While in college, I would take them out at Halloween and admire them again. Eventually, I looked for similar lanterns at thrift shops and, much later, on eBay. It became my hobby, and the search was captivating.

As an avid collector, I've done a lot of research on these lanterns. Papier-mache (pulp) holiday items were originally made in Germany in the late 1800s. American companies started manufacturing pulp lanterns in the 20th century. One of the biggest producers was F.N. Burt Co., a box-maker in Buffalo, New York. It molded and painted egg carton material, and then inserted a tissue face inside each lantern.

Dime stores sold the lanterns in the weeks before Halloween from the 1930s to the 1950s. Children used them to hold their candy while trick-or-treating. Some carried candles in them to guide them as they walked—I have a few lanterns with burned candle stubs in the bottom.

I was born in October, so I've always been a huge fan of Halloween and vintage Halloween items. I collect only original, intact and gently aged papier-mache lanterns. They give me joy. I often think of the children who carried them long ago and imagine their delight at receiving a lantern from their parents. How many of these do I own? I quit counting at 50.

Will Ogden • Wooster, OH

THEIR SPUTNIK CRASH-LANDED

Inventive mothers' homemade costumes were a smash.

In 1957, on most fall evenings, we stared at the skies from our front yards awaiting a glimpse of a Sputnik flyover. Our little town near Valley Forge, Pennsylvania, was infected with Sputnik fever as Halloween approached that year. The annual Malvern Halloween Parade offered a shiny silver dollar as first prize in several categories—a very big incentive for preteen entrants indeed.

My mother, Betty Selfinger DiLabbio, and my friend Linda Kay's mother, Marge Stanford Maxton, hatched a plan to create costumes for 8-year-old Linda and 10-year-old me. They brought down the biggest cardboard boxes from our attics—the ones that held our Christmas ornaments—spray-painted them silver, and cut holes in the bottoms for our heads to fit through. Our legs were then wrapped in aluminum foil. We wore hats made of aluminum pie plates with pipe cleaners poking through to represent antennae. Voila! Linda and I were SPUT and NIK, as labeled on our outfits!

Linda Kay weighed no more than a bag of potato chips and learned the hard way not to fall from a sudden gust of autumn wind when trapped inside a box: Without arms to break her landing, down she went, right in front of the judges' stand. Her hat launched like a flying saucer, and her tinfoil leg wrappings were shredded and torn asunder! Poor little SPUT cried her eyes out as our moms desperately tried to set her back up on her feet while an equally armless NIK ran in circles screaming, "Get up! Get up!" as the crowd laughed sympathetically yet maniacally at the entire scene.

Truth be told, we won the coveted first-place prize (each of us receiving our own silver dollar!). We never knew if it was in the Most Original or Comic Costume division. And our fathers grumbled for years at having to transport the Christmas ornaments down from the attic with flimsily covered holes in the bottom of those silly silver boxes.

Regina DiLabbio King • Malvern, PA

THE COMEBACK KID

*Her baby brother wasn't going to miss
Halloween three years in a row.*

Joey loved Halloween. When we were kids in the '50s, my little brother could not wait to get home, sort his candy into piles and eat all his favorites first.

When he was 8 he had to miss trick-or-treating because of a high fever. He pleaded with our mom for hours until he gave her a headache and was sent to his room in tears.

I went around the neighborhood with two bags, asking for treats for my brother who was home sick. The neighbors were very generous. But he didn't feel well enough to do his sorting and eating routine until the following weekend.

The next year Joey had two costumes ready: the pirate with an eye patch and a plastic sword that he was supposed to have worn the year before, and a new cowboy costume complete with boots and Lone Ranger six-guns that he'd gotten for his birthday. He was counting the days. But he came down with the flu and couldn't stand, never mind dress up and go out into the frigid New York night.

I went around with his sack and mine, and everyone said, "Not again!" Our kind neighbors poured goodies and change into Joey's bag, telling me, "He can buy what he likes when he gets better."

He had a sack full of candy and two dollars in change, but Joey wasn't happy.

When October came around again, Joey was ready. He had three unused costumes waiting to be worn, and he was a boy on a mission. My parents had already decided they had to let him go trick-or-treating no matter what.

Halloween fell on a Saturday that year, which gave Joey the chance to rest up so he could stay out late. He was the first one out and the last one home. When his bag got heavy he came home, changed his costume and started over again and again. Joey was determined to make up for lost

time. That night he was having the Halloween of his life.

When Joey, in his new Superman outfit, finally trudged in for the last time and saw his three bags of goodies waiting for the sorting, he hugged them and burst into tears of joy. Joey had won his battle with Halloween.

Josephine Mele • Moraga, CA

After two years of staying home on Halloween, all Joey wanted to do was trick-or-treat.

Car Ride with Vincent Price

In 1972, actor Vincent Price was the guest speaker at the University of South Alabama Halloween celebration. The next morning, I tagged along with my brother Billy as he drove Mr. Price to the airport. The setting was perfect: A heavy fog blanketed the city, the ancient oaks on Government Street dripped with Spanish moss, and dim lights shone in the windows of the old mansions. Mr. Price asked if they were funeral homes. We told him, "Not yet."

At the airport, everyone recognized him. I must admit, I had a smug look on my face as I walked next to him. And he was so tall! I even told him that. He looked down at me, then smiled and said, "Don't knock it, honey."

Because of the fog, his plane was delayed, so we had coffee and chatted about his art collection and his career. Billy asked him what it was like to work with Cecil B. DeMille. I chimed in, "Oh, that's right! You died in *The Ten Commandments*!" I then admitted that I had been in love with him

Mary (left) and a friend flank Mr. Van Ghoul himself.

since I was 10 years old. "Oh, all of 10 years," he said. I didn't tell him I was a 30-year-old housewife with three children. I just let him think I was a college student of 20!

Mary Burns Gresham • *Mobile, AL*

JUST YOUR IMAGINATION

In the mid-1980s, our teenage son needed a last-minute Halloween costume. I'm not a seamstress, but I had an idea. I bought about 7 yards of black cotton fabric, folded it in half lengthwise, laid it on the floor and had my son lie on it with his arms outstretched. With scissors, I cut from the bottom to make the gown part and then cut angled sleeves. Then I fashioned a hood for the top.

Over the years, different family members have worn the costume. Each time it's something different. Sometimes it's a ghoul, sometimes a monk—whatever the imagination can dream up.

Lynn Anderson • *Yakima, WA*

Good Deeds on Halloween

As a teenager in Helena, Arkansas, I worked for the local newspaper. On Thursdays we printed the eight-page *Shopping News*, and I had to bundle up the copies and get them to our carriers so they could deliver them the next morning.

In 1940, Halloween fell on a Thursday night. Millard Oldham, my very good friend and a Boy Scout, was helping me load up the car and make my deliveries. As we drove, we saw kids celebrating Halloween with harmless pranks. At one point we drove past a construction site and saw that the large A-frame sign with the contractor's name on it had been moved to the middle of the street.

If someone could move it that far, we could move it farther, we decided. So Millard, who was wearing his Boy Scout cap, got out of the car and headed for the sign while I pulled over to the curb.

When I got out and ran over to help Millard load the sign on top of my car, I found him talking to Clarence Bruce, the editor of the paper. We hurriedly revised our plan, carrying the sign back to the construction site and placing it where it rightfully belonged. As Millard and I drove away, we congratulated each other for doing such quick thinking.

The next afternoon all the carriers gathered at the office to pick up their papers. Mr. Bruce came down and handed Millard and me a copy. On the editorial page was a long article under the headline "Boy Scouts Help with Good Deeds." The story was all about two Boy Scouts going around town undoing the pranks of others.

Until now, no one other than Millard and I knew the true story.

Ralph L. Stewart • Highlands Ranch, CO

COSTUME CONTEST

In 1951, the teachers at Newburgh Elementary School encouraged all of us students to dress up for the school Halloween party. First through sixth graders would show off their costumes to seventh and eighth graders, who would vote for the grade with the best costumes. I'm the leopard in the photo of Mr. Bernie Newman's fourth grade class (circled).

The winning class got a big treat—a penny sucker. Back then, Halloween was about kids having fun. Wasn't it great when kids could be kids?

Jim Crawford • Newburgh, IN

Fourth graders at Newburgh Elementary School in Newburgh, Indiana, rose to the occasion on Halloween in 1951 when they competed with other classes for a best-costume award.

HEY DIDDLE DIDDLE...!

*The dish tried to run away with top prize
in this costume contest.*

It was 1949, a wonderful time to be a child in a small California town. Fathers had returned from the war, and families were putting their lives back together. Mothers often sewed Halloween costumes for their children at the time.

In our house, the question "What do you want to be for Halloween?" was a serious one. We gave a lot of thought to the answer.

My sister and I were blessed with a talented mother. Every year of our childhood, Mom worked with papier-mache, taffeta, paint and fabric to create our Halloween costumes. One year I was miraculously transformed into Minnie Mouse, complete with papier-mache mask, while my sister, Suzy, dazzled the block as a perfect Queen of Hearts.

The year 1949 stands out as the pinnacle of our mother's creativity. We were reading a lot of Mother Goose at the time, and I wanted to be the dish that ran away with the spoon from the rhyme "Hey Diddle Diddle." Suzy was to be the cat with the fiddle.

Mom and Dad worked together to create our costumes. They made the dish out of a mattress box cover and spent many late evenings gluing, cutting and painting.

Dad worked on logistics, such as how a small child could walk along the street inside the dish. His answer to the problem was to mount two handholds made of closet rods inside the costume. My parents were the perfect team.

At last all was ready, and it was time to get my head into the dish and walk to Whittier's Main Street for the town's parade and contest. But instead of appreciating the hard work my parents had done, I complained that the dish was heavy and that it kept slipping. It was stifling inside. Not to mention the thumping! Everyone, it seemed, had to thump the back of my costume.

After the parade proceeded up Main Street to the Whittier College campus, everyone milled about on the football field, admiring one another's costumes. We waited with anticipation for the judges' decision, who had finished looking over all the contestants.

Annie was the dish that ran away with the spoon while her sister, Suzy, was the cat and the fiddle.

We were all confident of a first-place finish for one of us—perhaps too confident. Imagine our shock when the coveted prize went to an ordinary angel! I was certain collusion was involved.

But once the dish was pulled over my head and I was free of the costume, my disappointment was somehow lessened. It felt so good to run and jump around on the grass with my sister and our neighborhood friends in their own costumes. In fact, we were already thinking about what we wanted to be next year.

As Suzy and I grew up, we became mothers and made costumes for our own children. Our memories of Mom's creative costumes are precious to us.

We've experienced the panic of a Halloween deadline. Somehow, the pace of life became more hectic in our generation, and we never seemed to have the time or talent to make anything as complex as the dish that ran away with the spoon or the cat and the fiddle. Fortunately, our kids never asked for a costume quite like it!

Annie Lawrie • Portland, OR

A Growing Tradition

The first autumn in our new home we invited the neighborhood kids to carve pumpkins into jack-o'-lanterns for Halloween.

After the excited children arrived, we rolled up the rug in the living room and covered the hardwood floors with newspaper. Then the kids carved the top out of each pumpkin. One by one each carver reached his or her hands deep inside the pumpkins and removed the seeds and guts. With a little coaching, they carved faces and designs that prompted broad smiles when a candle was placed inside. Then the kids proudly carried their jack-o'-lanterns outside, where we lined them up and lit the candles for a photo.

At the end of the night we rolled up the newspapers and added them to the compost bin along with the majority of the mess. That fun evening turned into an annual tradition that now involves both children and adults. Some years we have had as many as 40 friends, neighbors, co-workers and relatives attend.

After that first party I decided to experiment with the pumpkin seeds. I made a mound of dirt in the veggie garden and deposited the seeds deep in the middle, making sure they were covered. I ignored the spot all winter, and then to my pleasant surprise pumpkin plants appeared the following spring.

My first few years growing pumpkins didn't go very well. However, each year I learn something new and continue to plant the seeds from the pumpkin-carving party. Why not visit the garden center and sow the seeds of a pumpkin tradition in your own backyard?

S.J. Brown • Falling Waters, WV

IT WAS A HAPPY HALLOWEEN AFTER ALL

On October 31, 1978, our family moved from Chicago to a small town in Wisconsin. My husband, Jim, and I left behind our entire way of life to fulfill our dream of moving to the country and starting our own business.

The route took eight hours, straight north, and was uneventful except that each time we went through a town, my 6-year-old son, Ross, whined that he didn't get to go trick-or-treating.

Since we weren't able to leave until the moving truck had loaded up our furniture, we arrived at our new home around 10 p.m. As we were gaping up at the stars, a car pulled in the driveway.

The parents of the couple we were renting from had come over to check on us. They helped us carry in our suitcases and asked us about our trip. I said it had gone fine, except for missing trick-or-treating. With that, they left us to get settled.

About 15 minutes later there was a knock on the door. The sweet lady we had just met had two paper bags full of Halloween candy with our sons' names, Ross and Tim, written on them.

After she left, I said, "If this is the way country folks are, I'm gonna love it here." That was decades ago, and we are proud country people now.

Ann Koziol • Crandon, WI

THE LEGEND OF SKUNK HOLLOW

They braved the infamous headless horseman to visit their favorite neighbors down the road.

Halloween night found us kids scurrying along the dark, heavily wooded roads.

A full moon peeked around tall oaks and maples, sometimes illuminating the path before us, other times casting eerie shadows that both scared and thrilled us.

Trick-or-treating was difficult around our rural Pennsylvania farm because of long walks between houses. Kindly local farmers knew this. Instead of a quick exchange at the door, they invited us in to warm up around the wood stoves. They fortified us with big helpings of homemade goodies and fussed over our costumes.

The longest haul was along Hollow Road, from my house to the Kulp farm, but it was my favorite. In those days, though the road had no official name, we knew it as Hollow Road. Dad called it "Skunk Hollow" to tease his good friend Mr. Kulp, who lived at the end of it.

To us kids, it was the legendary Sleepy Hollow. We named it after the short story by Washington Irving featuring the fictional headless horseman character.

Five of us, ranging in age from 7 to 10 years old, were trick-or-treating together one particular Halloween. We scared ourselves silly by telling stories about the headless horseman, who surely lived in the woods.

As we neared the Kulp farm, we heard crashing and snorting among the trees. The sound of galloping hooves was headed straight for us. Frozen in fear, we were too scared to run. A creepy coldness ran up the back of my neck. Henry, age 7, finally broke the trance, running and screaming for all he was worth toward the Kulp farm. Seconds later, two deer leapt out right in front of us. After we caught our breath, we laughed about how little kids like Henry could be so scared of deer.

By the time we got to the house, Mrs. Kulp had calmed Henry. She herded us into her big farm kitchen and plied us with her delicious

Trick-or-treating was extra spooky on dark rural roads.

apple butter glazed donuts and fresh hot cider, all from their king and winesap apples. As we were leaving, she stuffed bags full of treats into our arms. Mr. Kulp saw that we were tired and insisted on taking us home. He broke a bale of hay into the bed of his pickup and covered us with some horse blankets. We arrived home filled with the warmth of good food and the knowledge that, as long as we had caring neighbors, we were safe from headless horsemen.

Pat Arbeiter • Grand Junction, CO

BEGGING FOR BISCUITS

Their giant dog just couldn't find the fun in Halloween.

A sea of cherub-faced princesses, ghosts and goblins raised jack-o'-lanterns and shouted "trick or treat!" We sat waiting for them outside. Marley, our komondor dog, was beside us, wagging his tail incessantly.

He loved little people. Despite his imposing size, most of them felt likewise. Often Marley found himself surrounded by neighbor children, their faces buried in his clumpy dreadlocks.

But that night, after the third or fourth Halloween salutation, Marley grew agitated. He watched anxiously, whimpering, as candy clunked into buckets and bags.

My husband and I didn't know what to make of it. The whining got worse, and eventually Marley crammed his huge head into a bag looking for treats. We replaced the candy, of course, and reprimanded him for his outburst. Marley simply plopped to the ground.

"Maybe we should put him in the house," I suggested.

"Let's give him another chance," my husband answered.

"Trick or treat!" a child cried, his feet crunching and crackling over the carpet of red, yellow, orange and brown leaves.

Marley sat up straight and tall. His eyebrows moved up and down and his enormous pink tongue remained frozen. Marley's eyes shifted from us to the child until we dropped the candy into the bag. He pawed the sack. He was looking for something.

"I know what the problem is," my husband said finally. "Trick or treat." I didn't get it, so he repeated the phrase, with the emphasis on treat. Then it hit me. Marley connected the word with doggy biscuits. He must have felt it was a really cruel prank, hearing that word over and over and watching kids run off with his booty.

I went inside, grabbed some biscuits and gave them to Marley. Outside, skeletons and pirates paraded across the yard, yelling the magic phrase.

We couldn't just train Marley to forget the word *treat*.

So every October, our former Halloween helper spends the night inside, waiting, like Scrooge at Christmas, for this unjust holiday to pass.

Lisa Mackinder • Kalamazoo, MI

Color Her Favorite Holiday Orange and Black

Halloween has always been my favorite holiday. Nearly every kid loves a holiday that results in a bag full of candy, but for me it goes much deeper.

I remember the moment that I realized I was a "Halloween person." I was visiting my grandmother's house, which sits at the end of a dead-end street and has a railroad track behind it. It must have been summer, one of those dark, rainy days made for indoor adventures. So my attention was drawn to the little desk in the doorway between the living room and what we called the "toy room."

The desk held a supply of construction paper in basic craft colors: red, green, orange and black. I was too young to be familiar with the calendar, so I asked my grandmother, "Which comes first, Halloween or Christmas?"

The answer was Halloween, so orange and black it was. And from that day forward the traditional imagery of pumpkins, witches, bats and owls that I crudely drew and cut from construction paper became special to me.

Pumpkins star in Helen's Halloween collection, which started decades ago after she cut her first witches, owls and bats out of construction paper.

As an adult, I have collected decorations from the past and notice the contrast between older designs and what is mass-produced today. When I was young, the stores seemed to turn orange and black with pumpkins and witches lining the shelves.

My decorations represent Halloween as an extension of autumn, with pumpkins as the focal point. My witches are not grotesque; rather, they resemble an old woman who might be interesting to know. To me, the fright aspect of Halloween should be left to the imagination, triggered by the rustle of dead leaves or a shadow across the moon.

Helen Mayne • Rochester, NY

SWEET TOOTH FIX

Do you long for the days of donning spooky costumes to solicit candy from neighbors? Take a delectable trip down memory lane.

CHOCOLATE CRAVINGS

This megaphone is mega-hungry! We'll bet you didn't know that Milky Way bars were actually named after malted milk shakes and not our solar system's brilliant galaxy.

'54

Cheer Leader!

Three-flavored sport from Mars' sunlit kitchens—the best-liked chocolate-covered candy bar in all the world . . .

Milky Way 5¢

* 1. Honest-to-Goodness MILK CHOCOLATE —from the finest imported chocolate beans
* 2. GOLDEN CARAMEL
* 3. CREAMY CHOCOLATE MALTED MILK NOUGAT

MARS Milky Way CHOCOLATE

PRESERVED BY
Life Savers

'62

LIFE SAVERS

The candy with the hole . . . still only 5¢

SMALL BUT SATISFYING

Life Savers wasn't kidding when it marketed its product as "the candy with the hole." In 1912, founder Clarence Crane punched holes in the center of his mints to make them stand out from similar candies of the era.

Pictures from the Past

HALLOWEEN

SCARY EXCITEMENT
Ghosts and goblins with treat bags in hand make a grand entrance at a Halloween party in 1960.

GUARDING THE CANDY
Mom and Dad went out to a Halloween costume party and I stayed home with my brothers Jeff (the clown) and Joe (the skeleton) to hand out the candy in 1957.

Greg Groom • *Columbus, OH*

GROUP FUN
Halloween shenanigans bring smiles to Joyce, Betty and myself, standing behind my sister Janie (in hood) and her friend Louise.

Kathleen "Kitty" Bowers • Warren, MI

DIAPER INGENUITY
Mom used cloth diapers to dress my older brother Lewis Young Jr. as a bunny for Halloween in 1944. Dad was serving as a Seabee in the South Pacific.

Connie Young Reeder • *Media, PA*

WALKING BEVERAGE
Dad made this for my sister Mary Susan, 10, in 1969 out of old ad displays from the liquor store where he worked.

Robert Hurley • *Baltimore, MD*

HANDLE WITH CARE
Here I am with a papier-mache jack-o'-lantern on my first Halloween in 1948. It's still my favorite holiday.

Julie Natale • *Centennial, CO*

TIGERS BY THE TAIL

I was living on the Clark Air Force Base in the Philippines in 1972 when I helped a seamstress make these fierce costumes for her sons Garth, Glenn and Ray.

Sue Jernigan • *Prattville, AL*

GHOULS' NIGHT OUT

In 1958 I was a witch carrying a big trick-or-treat bag. Here I am dressed up with Bette Bachand, Julie Rogers, Kathy Kale and Barbie Bachand.

Vicki Langwell
Albuquerque, NM

SEND IN THE CLOWNS!

I sewed all of these clown costumes for my daughters Sherry, Sandy, Sue and Sheila for Halloween in 1956.

Alice Gould • *Fulton, IL*

PURE BREAD

In 1947, I went to Green Street School. Mrs. Dunklee, our teacher, thought it would be great fun for us to make costumes from Wonder Bread wrappers for the Halloween parade. We scoured our neighborhoods, begging people to save the dotted wrappers for us. Mother sewed, stapled and pleated our one-of-a-kind costumes, and we thought up slogans for our signs. Marylin Brooks and I were the heels—that's me in the back with my mouth open.

June Anderson • *Brattleboro, VT*

ROLL WITH IT

My daughter Chelsea won a prize at school for her Charmin costume in 1985. Her earrings are miniature toilet rolls. We like to think Mr. Whipple would have approved.

Connie Young Reeder • Media, PA

GLAM SHOT

On Halloween night 1965, my friend Suzanne and I put on plastic wigs, tons of makeup and her mom's jewelry, and we went as Little Ladies. Oh, what fun we had.

Dara H. Gunnell • Pfafftown, NC

The Trick-or-Treat Retriever

Halloween resembles a national holiday—everyone seems to get in the spirit! Stores beckon buyers with an array of candy, glittering decorations and ghoulish costumes. Haunted-house themes illuminate neighborhood yards, and orange-and-black lights beckon callers. October 31 is a day for young and old.

Our furry four-legged friends also want to be part of the spooky antics. My golden retriever, Jonathan Douglass, was no exception. He was a real ham who loved Halloween. Johnny D, as I often called him, was a handsome guy with silky tan fur and big brown eyes framed by long lashes.

From his puppy years to his senior dog days, Jonathan joined the festivities and wore a costume. As a pup, he would fidget and pull off the hat and scarf that I had fashioned for him. Once he passed the terrible twos, he began playing along.

One year, Jonathan was an aviator and donned a scarf around his neck and a cap over his floppy ears. When he was 9, he was decked out as a rabbit wearing a ballerina's tutu. A pink ruffled jersey and soft satin ears rounded out his ensemble. The only thing he couldn't wear was toe shoes!

As a senior, Jonathan was the Wicked Witch of the West. Resplendent in his black hat and his cape bearing an embellished orange spider, he posed with a stoic look. The only thing missing: his broom.

Dressing in costumes was not the only part of Jonathan's Halloween. He loved to go out trick-or-treating. "John, you look fabulous," chuckled Gene, the salon owner. At our local bank, the children would get lollipops; Jonathan got Milk-Bones. Trick-or-treating would not be complete without a stop at the neighborhood deli, where the owner came out to see him: "Johnny, you look so good!" After a few slices of American cheese, it was time to head home. Jonathan was done trick-or-treating for another year. After supper, he trudged to his favorite spot, plopped down on the rug, let out a few yawns and went right to sleep.

Beverly Sce • Yardley, PA

Whether he was a pink ballerina rabbit or a wicked witch, Johnny D loved dressing the part!

RIGHT: ALEXIS GRATTIER/GETTY IMAGES

Ready, set, glow! On Halloween night, jack-o'-lanterns put on their
best faces and light the way for trick-or-treaters.

Thanksgiving Memories

Stories of togetherness, lovable grandparents,
feasts aplenty and recipes gone wrong are
sure to warm your heart.

GRANDMA HOSTED THE CROWD

There was always a warm welcome and plenty of gravy.

For my maternal grandmother, Thanksgiving was a huge event. With 26 grandchildren, she wanted room for everyone. The table ran through the dining room and into the living room, made a 90-degree turn, and ended in the parlor. Football fans sat where they could see the TV. People at one end couldn't see the people at the other! There were only two excuses for missing the event: for guys, if you had not yet bagged a deer, or for ladies, if you were in labor.

As each family arrived, my grandmother met us at the door in her apron with hugs and hellos using both our first and middle names. Her hugs could be suffocating. She was just so very glad to see each and every one of us and surely made us feel loved.

Her backyard was just the right size for a miniature football field, so while my mother, aunts and grandmother put the finishing touches on the meal and the guys checked out the game, we kids all went out to play in the cold. We were rough; it was tackle for sure, no sissy tag stuff for us. When we were called in, we were red-faced with running noses, and cries of "wash your hands" were heard from every mom.

My grandmother's pies were the highlight of the meal: pumpkin, mince, apple, cherry. When my new sister-in-law was attending her first gathering, she was puzzled when, during dessert, my uncle said, "Pass the gravy, please." She looked at me for help; I said, "For the pie." She had never seen anyone put gravy on pie before. It was something all my uncles had done as long as I could remember, and my dad and older brother had picked up the habit as well. I learned that my grandfather, who had died before I was born, had started the tradition. We all got a big chuckle at my sister-in-law's reaction, but after that, she was very happy to "pass the gravy" during dessert.

Mary L. Bos • *Tecumseh, MI*

NO STORE-BOUGHT CRANBERRY SAUCE FOR GRANDPA

A lot of love made it into the recipe.

The person who made Thanksgiving sparkle for my sister, my brothers and me was our paternal grandfather. Though our mother cooked a totally delicious meal, Grandpa stole the show with his special cranberry sauce.

Our grandfather Roy Van Ausdall started the tradition of making fresh cranberry sauce for Thanksgiving decades ago. His ruby-colored delight bears no resemblance to the jellied stuff that comes in a can. My siblings and I turned up our noses at the store-bought stuff!

One of my favorite memories of Grandpa is of him banging pots and pans around as he cooked in his tiny, old-fashioned kitchen. He had a way of making meals fun. For breakfast, he'd flip small silver-dollar pancakes in the air and catch them with a spatula. Of course, when mealtimes were over, he'd have used every dish, bowl and pot in the house, and being the oldest girl, I usually had to clean up.

On Thanksgiving Day at about 11:30, Grandpa would bound through the door of our home, wearing his gray fedora, a perfectly starched white shirt and a tie. He'd also be wearing his best grin as he belted out "Happy Thanksgiving!" to everyone in sight. With pride, he'd bring his best cut-glass bowl full of the delicious, garnet-colored cranberry sauce. The dish was given the place of honor—right next to the large, golden brown turkey.

As he grew older, he enlisted the help of my younger sister, Elaine. I can still see the scene. The kitchen in total chaos. Elaine at the huge single sink, washing and culling the round, plump berries. Grandpa in his crimson-stained apron, bending as he cranked the handle of the ancient black grinder, juice dripping onto the worn tile floor. Grandpa would mix with gusto. His thick white eyebrows would knit together in a frown as he tasted his creation. Turning his head to one side, he'd say, "I think we've hit it just right, Elaine! We're ready for turkey day."

Cheryle Van Ausdall Bryan • Valdosta, GA

WHEN THE WIND HOWLED

A sudden storm taught her the true meaning of Thanksgiving.

Thanksgiving 1938, I was a kid living in Plymouth, Massachusetts, the very spot where the Pilgrims had landed more than 300 years before. It was the perfect place to celebrate the holiday.

My mother and I lived with her best friend and her friend's husband, whom I called Aunt Jessie and Uncle Harry, and their two kids, Phyllis and Jerry. Mom and I shared a bedroom in the two-story house, which was not much more than a ramshackle cottage.

On Thanksgiving morning, I awoke to the delicious smell of cinnamon from the apple pies that my mom had baked earlier. Aunt Jessie had already cooked the turkey, and it was all brown and crisp.

A little later, Uncle Harry came into the kitchen and looked out the window. "It sure is blowing out there. The weatherman says we're in for a storm."

As we all sat down to dinner, the lights went out. The adults scrambled for extra candles and matches. They always kept a supply in the pantry. "And don't forget the flashlight on the shelf next to the candles!" Aunt Jessie called out.

The howling wind blew so hard through the cottage that it sounded like a freight train. The windows shook, and the tree branches banged against the side of the house. Then a driving rain started to fall. The storm was so noisy we had to yell to be heard.

We circled the dining room table, set the napkins on our laps, and took a moment for a silent prayer that this storm would pass by quickly.

"Somebody up there must have been watching over us," Mother said. "They waited for the turkey and trimmings to be done before they shut down our electricity."

As we gave a prayer of thanks, someone banged on the door. Uncle Harry opened it and found a police officer standing there. His rain gear made him look like he was wrapped in plastic.

"I'm sorry to tell you, sir, but you'll have to leave your house. We're evacuating everyone in the area," he said. "It's just too dangerous with the storm as bad as it is."

"But we were just sitting down to Thanksgiving dinner!" Aunt Jessie said.

"Wrap it up and take it with you," the officer replied. "You'll be picnicking at St. Mary's Church on Elm and Third."

We piled into the family Ford, our hungry stomachs growling, and drove through the pounding rain with the windshield wipers going at full tilt.

We had our Thanksgiving picnic on a blanket in the church rectory. We shared it with another family, the Smiths, who hadn't had time to bring theirs.

Phyllis and I whispered and giggled throughout the night. No one got too much sleep.

The storm passed during the night. It was said that the winds were up to 100 mph. On our way home, we passed uprooted trees, houses with the roofs blown off and water hydrants that looked more like geysers.

When we arrived, we were astonished to find that our home had disappeared. The wind had reduced our wooden cottage to a pile of splinters.

Uncle Harry, a soft-spoken, levelheaded man, was the first to say a word. "We may not have a roof over our heads, but we're all here and intact. For that I am extremely grateful."

We owed our lives to that police officer. If not for him, we would have been sitting around the dining room table celebrating our last Thanksgiving.

Bernice Applebaum • Carlsbad, CA

PASS THE GRAVY, MOM!

When I was young, our Thanksgiving and Christmas dinners were always held at Grandma and Grandpa Anderson's house. I used to tell my mom that Grandma was the "best cooker" in the world! My Aunt Bertha, Uncle Henry, and two cousins would always be there too. Uncle Henry was appointed to sit by me and my cousin Dolores to make sure that we behaved. That was a joke because he was the one who would get us giggling with his funny stories and comments!

There is one Thanksgiving meal that I will never forget. Grandma always served dressing, mashed potatoes and gravy with her yummy turkey dinners. My mom was the first person to pass the gravy. Guess what she did: She accidentally dumped the entire bowl of gravy on her plate! We all ended up passing her plate around so we could scoop off some of the gravy! To this day, I can still taste my grandma's delicious holiday dinners.

Nancy J. White • Omaha, NE

The Glory of the Grown-Up Table

My daughters Renee and Nadine and my nephew Tom always sat at a card table during holiday meals at my mom's house because the dining room table could not accommodate everyone. The three kids dubbed the dining room table the Grown-Up Table. The kids had the responsibility of setting up both tables, and never did we hear a grumble.

A few years ago, I found a Hallmark card depicting two boys sitting at a card table. The caption read: "When do you think we will be able to sit at the grown-up table?" I mailed one to each of the "kids" (now in their 40s), and we all had a good laugh about it when we assembled at my sister's for Thanksgiving.

The highlight was when we asked the kids what they were whispering about as they sat at that little card table all those years ago. They looked sheepishly at one another as they confessed that they were planning our demise so that they could sit at the Grown-Up Table! Plan as they might, they never could decide who would be the first one eliminated.

Memories are wonderful.

Carol Macek Martinichio
Binghamton, NY

Thanksgiving Dinner

Back in the '40s, my mom always made a turkey with meat stuffing for our dad and us six kids. One year she decided to try a bread stuffing, since she'd heard that a lot of other moms were happy with it. We did not appreciate her efforts! And that was the last time she made "something different." But ever since, through all the decades that I've been married, bread stuffing is the only one I've used. Go figure!

Johanna Vitale Dosky

This picture reminds me of Thanksgiving, and those memories are dear to me: Pies being made. Breaking the wishbone with my brother. Mom's side dishes. Setting the table. Enjoying this annual tradition and waiting for the ones to follow in the coming years.

Elaine Wafford Currie

I remember dinners at my grandma's—she had a big wood cookstove that made the whole house hot. You had to go out on the back stoop to pump water for drinking and cooking. She even had a phone you had to crank to make a phone call. You went into the parlor only on special occasions. I loved spending the night and sleeping in her big feather bed. I miss my grandma and everything about her.

Gracie Poyer

I was 60 when my mom passed, and I had never cooked a turkey, because both Thanksgiving and Christmas had always been at my parents' house! It was wonderful. The warm feeling wasn't from the dinner—it was the love.

Sheridan Fenwick

It was the night before Thanksgiving. Oh, the smells being stirred up in that kitchen. Pies baking. Motown playing. Me waiting for them beaters so I could lick them. Sniff... Oh, what's that, now? A Mardi Gras party cake? Then to wake up and smell that turkey cooking. Oh, yes, it's *Thanksgiving*.

Angel Davis Powers

MUMS BRIDGE THE MILES

Their friendship grew like the flowers he shared years ago.

Raymond, my Army buddy at Fort Dix, New Jersey, in the 1960s, spoke with a soft Kentucky drawl, while I was a fast talker from a Jersey suburb. It took us a while to crack the speech barrier, but once we did, we became close friends.

During one particular leave Raymond invited me to come home with him to Campbellsville, in tobacco country, where I met his family and his fiancee, Laura.

He showed me his hometown's claims to fame: the Fruit of the Loom underwear factory and a small liberal arts college. I liked the area, the friendly people, and Campbellsville College. In fact, after my stint in the Army, I enrolled there. Raymond, by then a married man, helped settle me in my new dorm.

That fall of 1968, classes were in full swing and Thanksgiving was fast approaching. There wasn't time for me to drive home, and holiday airfares proved prohibitive. I envisioned eating a Big Mac for my holiday meal.

Then Raymond stopped by to say, "George, we'd love for you to join us for Thanksgiving dinner."

Thanksgiving Day dawned cool and crisp, with deep blue skies. I didn't want to arrive empty-handed, so I brought a rust-colored chrysanthemum plant that I thought would make a handsome centerpiece.

Nestled near a ridge, Laura's family farm had a clapboard house, a weathered barn and acres of sweet corn and burley tobacco, among other crops. A stream gurgled nearby and roosters crowed in this little piece of paradise.

When I handed Laura's mom the plant, she exclaimed, "My, oh my!" She must have read my mind because she set it in the middle of the table.

After the turkey was carved, we all held hands around the table, Norman Rockwell style, and bowed our heads as Raymond said grace: "For each morning with its light, for rest and shelter of the night, for health and food, for love and friends, for everything thy goodness sends."

The meal was delicious, and Laura's mom made sure I took leftovers.

Months turned into years, and after graduation I drove out to the farm to say goodbye. It wasn't easy. After hugs, handshakes and a salute from Raymond, I sped off.

Every Thanksgiving since then, my Army buddy and I have exchanged "across the miles" cards, each recalling something special about holidays together and holidays apart.

Laura's mom planted the rust-colored mum next to her house, where it produced scads of showy flowers each autumn. She later divided it, giving new plants to neighbors along with the story of its Thanksgiving origin.

Both Raymond and I are retired from teaching now. "It's hard to believe that we've been sending Thanksgiving cards for decades!" I wrote to him recently. "How's the chrysanthemum doing? Does it still come back every year?"

He answered back, "I'll say! I fertilize it, pinch out new growth, mulch in winter and divide it, and it continues to flourish."

But we suspect that these aren't the only reasons the mum has prospered. It has thrived because of love, friendship and a bond that stretches across time and distance.

George Flynn • Newton, NJ

SIX GENERATIONS OF NANA DILLON'S STUFFING

A family enjoys a holiday specialty and passes along the tradition.

The smell of sage dressing takes me back to my grandma's kitchen. She was, to me, very old and very wise. My memory of Nana's kitchen at Thanksgiving time is so poignant. Her name was Elizabeth Dillon. She was from Ireland, and she had it even harder than most immigrants. Her husband died and left her with a 2-year-old boy and newborn twins. My mom was one of the twins. Elizabeth's life was one of "making do," as the expression goes. She had so very little.

Her sage dressing might make it seem that she had an abundance of food. That was not the case at all! She made a living by sewing and often bartering for goods. In this manner, she obtained the necessary ingredients for her famous stuffing. It is difficult in this day and age to fathom no Social Security, medical care or food stamps. On the other hand, back in those days, no one expected any help.

She often talked to me about the dressing as she made it. It took her back to Ireland, her parents and her 13 siblings. My mom, Olive, joined in many times as we prepared for holidays. What fun it was to grind the celery, onions and giblets. We had to place the old-fashioned grinder on the counter and tighten it like a skate key. It was a mess, but we all laughed (and cried because of the onions) and talked as we cleaned up. Nana would say, "Small cubes, girls," when we were preparing the bread. We cut off the crusts and put them outside to feed the birds.

Left to right: Joyce; her daughter, Kathleen; her granddaughter, Kristen; and her great-granddaughter, Lucia; Joyce's grandmother Elizabeth Dillon; Joyce's mother, Olive G. McDonald (and what an uncanny family resemblance).

Today I have passed on Nana's dressing recipe to my daughter, Kathy, and her daughter, Kristen. Kristen has recently given birth to a baby girl named Lucia. We all have honored my grandmother with our middle name of Elizabeth! Hopefully, Lucia Elizabeth will be passing on the famous stuffing recipe to her children someday!

Joyce E. Spotts • *Kenmore, NY*

SIDE-SPLITTING TIME

A frugal decision turned one turkey day into an unforgettable holiday.

When Thanksgiving comes around, I always remember a funny one that happened years ago when my husband and I were a young married couple stationed at an Air Force base in Albuquerque.

My brother-in-law and his wife, Pat, were going to join us for the holiday in our very small apartment. My sister-in-law had won a large turkey from her place of work. It was much too big for four people, so we decided to cut it in two. We'd cook one half for the dinner and freeze the other.

A few days before Thanksgiving, my husband told me he had invited a young couple who had just been transferred to the base. They were new to Albuquerque and had no family here. Pat and I thought that half a turkey might not be enough for six of us. And besides that, it would look rather strange on a platter. So we retrieved the frozen half of the turkey, and in a panic we quickly thawed it and carefully sutured the two halves together.

On Thanksgiving, the roasted bird came out of the oven looking picture perfect— golden brown and juicy. Pat and I were pleased with ourselves. No one would know about our handiwork.

All went well until we sat down at the cramped dinner table and someone bumped it. We looked on in horror as the stitches gave way and the turkey halves separated to each side of the platter, revealing a mound of dressing that stood there like a small mountain. The shocked looks on all our faces were priceless; I wish we'd had a camera nearby.

Pat finally broke the stunned silence when she said, "That worked out well, just liked we planned it!" We burst out in laughter, filled our plates with turkey and all the fixings and had a wonderful dinner.

I often wonder if that young Air Force couple ever remember that "parting-of-the-ways" turkey.

Lorraine Seals • *Bosque Farms, NM*

LEFT: STEVE BJÖRKMAN

A FEAST TO REMEMBER

You can take all you want, but make sure to eat it!

Francis in his uniform; the ship upon which he served in the Pacific.

n 1944, while serving aboard a subchaser, the USS *PC-606*, in the Pacific war zone, we ate meals that were only as special as our cook (whom we called Pops, due to his advanced age of 32) could make them with our dehydrated food. But Thanksgiving Day was a lucky day indeed. Our captain had received permission for the *606* crew members to eat Thanksgiving dinner at the Guadalcanal Navy base mess hall, which was second to none.

Early that afternoon, we headed across Iron Bottom Sound (so called because of the number of American, Japanese and Australian ships that had been sunk there) and anchored in the harbor. The hungry crew joined the long lines of service personnel at the chow hall, but the wait was well worth it. There was roast turkey with all the trimmings, ham, sweet and mashed potatoes, all manner of vegetables, and great desserts. It was a sight you wouldn't believe. They even had real hard-boiled eggs. (I dreamed of one sunny-side up; all we ever saw in our mess hall for breakfast was those scrambled dehydrated eggs, along with dehydrated potatoes and gritty powdered milk.) Needless to

say, we ate until we were stuffed. As always with the Navy, there was a prominent sign above the serving line that said, "Take all you want, eat all you take." We were even able to take a short walk around the area to let the main meal settle down in our stomachs, making room for another go at that wonderful chow.

One thing that didn't change, no matter how great the food, was the little weevils in the bread due to the damp tropics. All grains had these ever-present critters. It was either pick out the weevils or skip the bread. A case of choosing "the lesser of two weevils," you could say. Excuse the pun! Weevils or not, it was the best Thanksgiving dinner and the best meal we had enjoyed since we'd left the States in November 1943, and we had much to be thankful for.

Francis J. Mahoney • Casselberry, FL

HER FAVORITE FAMILY

Lasting memories were made when they were all together.

"They're here! They're here!" I screeched as I heard the car door slam.

From the late '40s to the mid-'60s, our fully cooked Thanksgiving turkey arrived each year via car at 11 a.m. sharp, accompanied by my favorite aunt, uncle and cousin—Aunt Norma, Uncle Earl and Richard!

Aunt Norma woke up at 4 a.m. to cook the turkey before the annual trek from Seymour, Connecticut, to Staten Island. Mom prepared the potatoes, green and orange vegetables, and pumpkin pie.

Before dinner, we chatted and laughed while Mom and Aunt Norma "slaved away" in the kitchen. In reality, we heard much laughter coming from their direction as well.

Uncle Earl huddled in front of the small TV upstairs to watch as many football games as he could before dinner. When the dinner bell rang, we all gathered around the dining room table, which was covered in a white lace tablecloth. "For our blessings and what we are about to eat, and for what Suzie has already eaten, let us be thankful," prayed my ever-witty dad.

The moans and groans began as everyone finished his or her second helping. As always, Richard and I scooped the roasted marshmallows off the untouched sweet potatoes, wondering why Mom didn't just bake the marshmallows.

"Sweet potatoes are traditional Thanksgiving food," Mom steadfastly insisted.

After the meal, the kids hit the kitchen. We mixed water, flour, sugar and salt into moist masses that we put into bags. We couldn't wait to turn off the living room lights.

"Shut your eyes and put your hand in," we instructed the adults.

"That's pigs' guts," we continued.

To our delight, all the adults reacted as we'd hoped, with an "eew" or an "ick" or a squeal. At seven years old, I actually thought we'd fooled them.

Forty years later, upon receiving an urgent phone call from Richard and his wife, Cara, I boarded a plane to Connecticut with hopes of seeing my favorite aunt one last time.

"She waited for you," said Richard, as we hugged, tears in our eyes.

Above: parents, Sherwood and Alice Seeley, and Aunt Norma and Uncle Earl Overton, Grandmother Bessie Seeley, Suzanne, brother Robert, and cousin Richard; Right: Suzanne ready for turkey!

Two days later, she died, early on Thanksgiving morning. Family members prepared a huge turkey dinner that day in her honor. As the dining table wouldn't hold all of us, the teenagers chose to eat from TV tables in the living room, watching all the football games they possibly could, while my cousin and I scooped the marshmallows off the sweet potatoes.

After all, it was tradition.

Suzanne G. Beyer • Bothell, WA

THE FOUR-LEGGED TURKEY

In 2003, I thought I'd trick my young granddaughter with a four-legged turkey. I made two slits near the legs and shoved one extra leg on each side. When she came over, I pulled the pan out and showed her. She was in awe! We took photos, and then we showed our special turkey to our guests, who were "amazed." However, when my granddaughter returned to kindergarten, the teacher told her that there was no such bird. She was so sad! I gave her a newspaper article to take to school. It reported the birth of a four-legged duck and said that every now and then, four-legged turkeys and chickens are born too. My little joke was saved! Every year now, I have a four-legged turkey, to everyone's amazement.

Sylvia Hughes • Noblesville, IN

Gathering at Gramma's

We always looked forward to Thanksgiving dinner at Gramma's house, and 1949 was no different. Gramma and Grampa Dell lived, literally, over the river and through the woods, as Grampa was a logger. They lived near Walton in the Coast Range of Oregon. Their house was a "company house," owned by the logging outfit Grampa worked for as the "bull of the woods," that is, the logging foreman. Because it was a distance from our house to theirs, we made it a weekend visit, though dinner was always a sumptuous spread on Thursday. Our family group for that holiday wasn't large: my grandparents, my parents, my two older siblings, and an uncle and aunt. Gramma had also invited a couple of neighbors who would have been alone otherwise.

The kitchen was a long, narrow affair with a breakfast nook at one end and on the other end a door opening into the "formal" dining room, which contained the big dark-wood table, made longer by the extra leaves Gramma put in for special occasions. From the sideboard she would pull the table pad and a starched, clean white tablecloth and put both on the table. To a little girl, it looked like a snowy blanket—and indeed, some years, there was already snow in the mountains.

Thanksgiving morning we woke to the smell of frying bacon. When we were visiting, we slept in the two upstairs bedrooms that were directly over the kitchen. Gramma would open the heat grates in the ceiling so some heat could come up to those bedrooms, and along with that heat came the wonderful smell of bacon frying on the wood stove. She had two ranges in her kitchen but much preferred the wood over the electric. As the day progressed and she worked, with family help, dinner was slowly cooked and assembled for serving. Being small, I couldn't do much. In spite of the fact that I was right in the way, Gramma always let me open the cupboards and drag out pans to play with, allowing me to cook my own dinner...at least in my imagination. My mom would try to stem that activity, but Gramma always intervened on my behalf.

As the table was loaded with all that good food, chairs were pulled up. In addition to those from the dining-table set, more chairs came from the breakfast nook, and sometimes we also used Gramma's sewing stool from her bedroom. And at last, we would sit down to a meal truly fit for a king.

Molly G. Smith • Sandy, OR

IT'S RAINING TURKEYS

*Their local farm store manager meant well, but he
overestimated a turkey's aerial abilities.*

The most memorable day of 1950—
as well as any other year I can think
of—in the little town of Dunkirk,
Indiana, arrived just before Thanksgiving.

Mr. LeFevre, manager of the Clover Farm
Store, decided to give away some turkeys.
But he wanted to do something different
that year instead of the usual raffle. So he
ran an ad in *The Dunkirk News*: The Saturday
before Thanksgiving at 2 p.m., he would
throw live turkeys off the roof of the store.

I walked downtown about half an hour
before the specified time so I wouldn't miss
a second of this exciting event. A huge crowd
(for Dunkirk) had already assembled, eagerly
awaiting the big turkey giveaway. Everybody
was talking at once and making quite a din
when Mr. LeFevre suddenly appeared up on
the roof of his building.

The crowd gave a big cheer as he stepped
to the edge of the roof. He'd lined up six large
wooden crates behind him, and he pointed
to them as he made a short speech that no
one could hear because he was too high up
off the ground. Everyone applauded anyhow
when he stopped talking and reached into
one of the boxes.

The look of gleeful anticipation on people's
faces quickly turned to panic when the live
turkeys, their wings outstretched and feet
spread out in front of them like eagle talons
began to plummet to the ground like crazed
dive bombers.

Mr. LeFevre was up there pitching them
off the roof one right after the other, and
he must not have noticed that people down
below were screaming and shoving to get
out of the way of the terrified birds.

I did see Chester Schlegle manage to catch
one, and everybody was glad for him. Times
had been tough for his family, and a nice, fat
turkey would definitely brighten up their
Thanksgiving dinner.

I'm not sure where the rest of the dive-
bombing birds ended up. Looking back, I
hope a kindly local farmer adopted them and
took them back to his farm where they lived
out their lives away from such foolishness.

When we got home, Grandpa noted,
"At least the turkeys weren't frozen. He
could've killed somebody." For several
weeks after that, it seemed like Mr. LeFevre
kept to himself a little more than usual.
But really, nobody held "the day it rained
turkeys" against him. We all knew his
intentions were good.

James Wood • *Smithville, TN*

MYSTERY MEAT

*Between the stuffing and the pumpkin pie,
there was still room for a surprise.*

My husband and I had only recently joined the Navy civilian service in November 1943. It was our first Thanksgiving stationed in Clearfield, Utah, and as newlyweds from Texas, we didn't have any relatives living nearby. However, we often shared rides to work with a nice man named Ralph. After hearing we would be spending Thanksgiving alone, he invited us to celebrate the holiday with his family.

We arrived at his house early in the afternoon on Thanksgiving Day, thinking we might help with some chores before the meal was served. Ralph's eldest daughter answered our knock at the door, still in her pajamas, and called for her dad. Ralph was really flustered and admitted he'd forgotten to tell his wife he'd invited us for dinner.

His wife, though she was embarrassed that she and her family had overslept, insisted we stay. Other relatives were bringing most of the food, but Ralph's wife hadn't yet bought the turkey she had promised to serve. When the extended family began to arrive, Ralph, my husband and three of Ralph's nephews got in a car and drove to Ogden to shop for a turkey. After two long hours, they finally returned.

Ralph handed me a big brown sack full of meat and told me to start frying.

Fried turkey? I'd never heard of frying turkey.

But I did as I was told and began to flour and fry the turkey pieces. I'd never seen so many thighs and drumsticks from a single turkey. Ralph explained that there were no more whole turkeys left at the market, so he'd bought some turkey parts. The butcher had told Ralph to fry them and they would turn out all right.

The rest of Ralph's family showed up, all bringing wonderful dishes of food and pie. Finally, the turkey was all fried, and the meal was set and ready to eat. We said grace and began our very tasty, filling meal.

After the main course was over, we sat down to enjoy a cup of coffee and some pie. Ralph asked his mother how she liked the meat she'd had for dinner. She said she'd never tasted fried turkey before, but it was really good. Ralph asked everyone if they had

The fryer and the rabbit buyer, Bettie and Ralph, in 1958.

liked the meat. Everyone agreed that it had been delicious, though they'd never had fried turkey before, either.

Ralph laughed and said, "Well, you still haven't had fried turkey—it was fried rabbit!"

After taking in our shocked expressions, Ralph revealed that by the time he'd gotten to the market to buy the turkey, rabbit was the only meat left. He bought it all.

That day in Clearfield, 22 people enjoyed a very unusual Thanksgiving dinner.

Bettie Shute • Walla Walla, WA

FIVE MONTHS OF PLANNING

*Holiday season began in mid-July when Grandma-Ma
fired up the canning stove in her summer kitchen.*

Preparations for Thanksgiving began early on my family's sheep ranch in Northern California's Anderson Valley. While my cousin and I were riding our ponies over the dry, grassy hills and swimming in the Navarro River, Mother, Grandma-Ma, Auntie Gert and my older cousins began the annual ritual of canning in the old homestead's summer kitchen.

The summer kitchen filled one end of a long enclosed back porch. It had a counter with a white porcelain sink; cupboards cluttered with canning pots, sieves and funnels; a worktable covered with checkered oilcloth; and an ancient wood stove. A large pantry with shelving stood just beyond the old stove's brick firewall.

By mid-July, the summer kitchen was running full steam—literally! Peas were always the first to be processed. Everyone Grandma-Ma could recruit sat on the back porch steps shelling the peas into large pans as we wished we were out swimming. Then came the cherries. Grandma-Ma and Mother packed them into pint jars, while Aunt Gert separated the riper cherries into a large pot to be made into a delicious jam, which to this day is my favorite.

Peaches and apricots followed shortly. Apricots only needed to be washed, pitted and packed into jars. Peaches, the family's favorite, were carefully blanched in the old black enamel kettle, then skinned, halved and packed. They were stored in a place of honor in the center of the pantry, shimmering golden in the light of the room's sole 100-watt bulb.

Then came the string beans, corn, cucumbers, beets and two giant Red Wing crocks stuffed with shredded cabbage slowly fermenting into sauerkraut. After all the tomatoes were canned and the late summer apples stored, my cousin Skip and I helped Grandma-Ma and Aunt Gert hang bouquets of fragrant oregano and lavender high on the pantry walls. By fall, ropes of onions and garlic hung at the ends of the shelves, and crates of apples, potatoes, squash, pumpkins and walnuts lined the floor.

I loved helping Grandpa search for the perfect branch of California bay leaves to hang over the

Ray's family gathers to enjoy Thanksgiving at the old farmhouse in the late '40s.

pantry door, which he believed kept away the bugs. The bay leaves also found their way into Grandma-Ma's winter soups and stews.

When the November rains came, Grandma-Ma filled the remaining shelf space with Folgers coffee cans packed with her famous fruitcakes—along with a bottle of brandy for the finishing touch. The pantry's aroma of spices, apples and bay leaves drifted into the house, announcing the Thanksgiving season.

The weekend before Thanksgiving, our aunts, uncles and cousins began to arrive, and we all took up temporary residence in the five upstairs bedrooms and an old cabin in the redwood grove behind the house. My uncles helped Grandpa catch up on repairs around the ranch; my aunts baked every conceivable type of pie and bread; and we cousins played checkers, card games and Monopoly in the front room, clustering as close to the warm wood stove as possible.

With four leaves extending the dining table into the front room, Grandpa would say grace, thanking God for the bounty stored in the barn and in the back-porch pantry, which smelled of spices, apples, California bay leaves and a hint of brandy.

Ray Prather • Rochester, MN

New Tradition

Holiday dinners at Grandma's were grand affairs, with delicious food, her best china, a beautiful centerpiece and plenty of lively conversation. Thanksgivings were no exception, and Grandma's table would be loaded down with all the fixings. For dessert, we always had pumpkin pie with whipped cream.

One Thanksgiving, Grandpa decided to play a joke on us grandchildren. He put whipped cream on his mashed potatoes, then poured gravy on his pumpkin pie. He dug in as if they were the most delicious things he had ever tasted. We all decided to try it, too, since Grandpa seemed to be enjoying his so much.

The whipped cream with mashed potatoes wasn't so good, but Grandpa's joke backfired—we really liked the gravy and pumpkin pie combination! Though our grandparents are gone now, we still enjoy the unusual Thanksgiving treat that Grandpa first introduced to us.

Brenda Mitchell • Sheffield, AL

A TURKEY SURPLUS

I was a junior officer serving aboard the USS *Wainwright* in November 1944 when we ran into a hurricane.

The high winds and heavy seas damaged our ship, so we were forced to dock on Thanksgiving Day at the Brooklyn Navy Yard, where Red Cross workers served us a turkey dinner. I was grateful but in a hurry, as I'd been given leave. I wolfed down the turkey and hustled to catch a plane bound for Cleveland. I bet you can guess what the airline served us for dinner.

With two turkey dinners under my belt, I met my wife downtown. She'd waited for me to have dinner, so we sat in a restaurant and had (choke) turkey! It would be a long time before I could eat turkey again.

Robert Lechner • Berea, OH

READY TO DINE

The last time we celebrated Thanksgiving at my parents' home in Minnesota was in 1961. I'm in the back row on the right. Somehow we managed to get all of us seated around the table. My dad loved carving the turkey almost as much as we loved eating it!

Gloria Coleman • Fridley, MN

VINTAGE ADS

THANKSGIVING ALTERNATIVES

Let someone else handle the cooking.

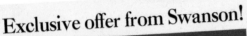

'62

GUILT-PROOF OF PURCHASE

Though sales of Swanson TV dinners soared as convenience food was starting in 1954, few would equate them with home-cooked meals. Here, Swanson provides a handy excuse for anyone feeling guilty about serving a frozen turkey dinner at Thanksgiving: Get a classy writing set when you buy two.

'64

STAR POWER AT HOJO'S

This ad plays on singer Rudy Vallee's star turn as corporate boss J.B. Biggley in the popular musical *How to Succeed in Business Without Really Trying*, which ran on Broadway from 1961-'65. Vallee reprised his role for the 1967 movie.

ye Indians are hungry tonight! Be a friendly Pilgrim and serve your little tribe a real turkey dinner. Besides tender slices of succulent turkey, there's old-fashioned dressing, fresh-tasting peas, and mashed potatoes. Expensive? Indeed, no! Just *tastes* expensive!

thank g♥♥dness for

Banquet®
frozen foods

Banquet Turkey DINNER

Banquet Beef DINNER
Banquet Fried Chicken DINNER
Banquet Ham DINNER

'64

FAST AND CHEAP

Frozen dinners came of age in an era when women were entering the workforce at a steady clip. Here, Banquet wisely markets to the busy working mom pulled in a dozen directions, for whom what mattered most was getting those little bellies full quickly and cheaply.

Pictures from the Past

THANKSGIVING

LET'S EAT!

Grandpa Henry Walker is at the head of the table behind the mashed potatoes; I'm right beside him. Grandma Cora, who did all the cooking and rarely sat down, took this photo in her dining room in Chamois, Missouri, in 1963.

Glenda Ferguson • Paoli, IN

TABLE IS SET

A holiday dinner in '64 was a good time to bond with my dad, Roy.

Sidney Hepler • Sunrise, FL

HAPPY MEAL

Uncle John Court took this picture of family members finishing up a turkey dinner in the 1950s.

Carl Vincent • *Medical Lake, WA*

KID PILE!

I'm holding the beach ball. I was crammed onto my grandma's sofa with my two brothers and six cousins on Thanksgiving. Every year the Richards clan traveled from several states to be together at Grandma's.

Gary Richards

ALL TOGETHER NOW

My cousin Glenn Brown of Evansville, Indiana, captured this photograph of the family gathered at the piano during one holiday in 1951.

Nellie Jane Rust • *Newburgh, IN*

Linda's family, though small, made a big deal of holidays in the 1960s.

THE TRIPOD IS UP...

Let the celebration begin!

Being a military family meant that we spent most of our holidays away from extended family. Thanksgiving was my dad's favorite day of the year, and my parents always made it special.

Preparations started early and with a bustle. I was allowed to sleep in, but my mother set an alarm for herself. My father, usually a late sleeper, was up early, too.

In the week before, Mom polished the silver and wrapped it in plastic so it wouldn't tarnish. She ironed the embroidered linen tablecloth, but didn't put it on the table until it was time. And she created a simple centerpiece with fresh flowers, fall leaves and a twig or two. When I create a centerpiece now, I take photos of it—not because it's extraordinary, but because I'm not sure I'll ever be able to make another one like it. My mother, on the other hand, was never at a loss.

While Mom was busy in the kitchen, Dad gathered the movie camera, film and cables, and found the perfect location for the tripod. He'd always request that we make a practice walk down the hall and into the dining room—a rehearsal so he could be sure the tripod was positioned at the perfect angle.

Mom and I obliged, giggling as he pretended to be a tyrannical movie director—never mind that he was still in his pajamas. We knew how much he loved this part of Thanksgiving.

Once the turkey had been basted for the final time and the tripod was in place, it was time to change into what my mother called our finery—and to start the festivities.

As I look back, it's remarkable to me that my parents went to all of that effort just for the three of us. They treated each holiday and celebration as if it was a big deal, because our family was more about love and togetherness than numbers. For that, I'll always be thankful!

Linda Russon McDonel • Tustin, CA

"When we finally arrived at my grandparents' house, they would run out to meet us. I think their excitement rivaled mine! Here, four generations of Heplers gather around the Thanksgiving table in 1975. I'm in the center."

Cami Hepler • Hickory, NC

Christmas Festivities

Remember department store Santa visits? How about the best gift you ever received? Take a walk down Christmas memory lane.

A Wish Book of Memories

On a Thanksgiving morning in the mid-'60s, while my mother was busy in the kitchen, she threw a book at my brother and me to distract us and keep us out of her way. She said, "Here—look through this and see if there's anything you guys want for Christmas."

The book was the Sears Christmas catalog. It kept us occupied for hours that morning, and a ritual was born. Every Thanksgiving, with the

Macy's parade on the TV, my brother and I would sit on the living room floor with pen, paper and the Sears wish book.

Feeling nostalgic, I recently went looking for a 1968 wish book. I chose 1968 because I was then 11 and my brother was eight—great ages for boys and toys. And '68 was the year Sears renamed its Christmas supplement catalog *America's Favorite Wish Book*. Thank goodness for eBay. I won the online auction, and on a chilly November day, my 1968 wish book came in the mail, much as it would've been delivered 47 years ago.

When I opened the package, it was 1968 again. I couldn't put it down!

The catalog contained everything from A to Z—from accordions and ant farms to zip-up sweaters and zebra-print bedspreads. Each item was expertly photographed and accompanied by well-written copy. I could almost imagine Don Draper hovering over a bottle of Brut or English Leather cologne, writing the line "The distinctive scent that's always civilized but never quite tame."

The prices were equally entertaining. A package of two D-cell batteries was 38 cents, and a ceramic ashtray with your family coat of arms sold for $2.79. Other prices were unexpectedly high. Since the median household income in 1968 was less than $9,000, how difficult it must have

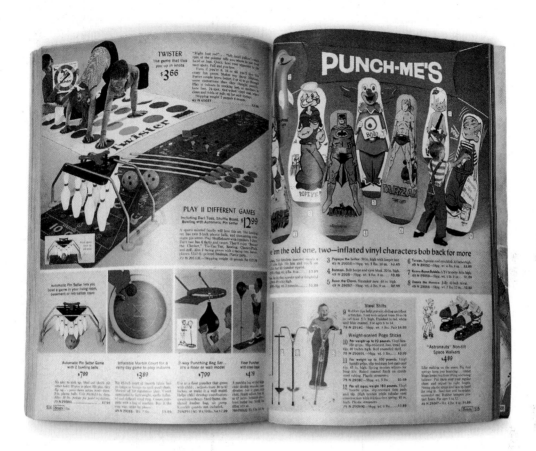

been to afford a 23-inch color TV for $629.95 or an electric typewriter for $237.95.

Turning to the toy section was like opening the door to Santa's workshop. Toys and games like Lincoln Logs ($3.88), Operation ($3.99), Time Bomb ($3.19), Rock 'em Sock 'em Robots ($9.99), the Hot Wheels Double-Dare Drag Set ($6.88), and Spirograph ($2.93) had all made it from the pages of the wish book to a spot under our family's Christmas tree.

But the page that I stared at the longest time was page 505, with the GI Joe space capsule and suit. GI Joe and his accessories (what boy didn't have Joe's footlocker?) often led to conflicts on Thanksgiving morning when my brother and I saw the same toy in the catalog at the same time. The disagreement was generally settled in

Sears, already famous for its iconic mail-order catalog, produced its first Christmas catalog in 1933. Mike shared this 1968 Sears wish book with us.

one of two ways—either I'd put my brother in a headlock until he said "uncle," or my father would yell from behind his newspaper, "If you two don't knock it off, you'll get a couple Barbies instead of GI Joes."

As I thumbed through the colorful pages, I realized that I wasn't looking at just an old catalog—more like a family album or a high school yearbook. The pages didn't hold merchandise; they held memories. The wish book was a 605-page time capsule, and I was lucky enough to open it.

Mike McCrobie • Oswego, NY

Getting the Big Book

The Sears catalog had a hand in shaping America's Christmas traditions, and its influence endures in surprising ways.

By Natalie Wysong

PARIS ISN'T CALLING

The company's products weren't fashion-forward, but their presentation was influential. Catalog designs reflected popular looks and put city style within reach.

DOWN ON THE FARM

Sears' early general catalogs took hold in places with few shops and stores. Filled with merchandise for farm families, the catalog quickly became a staple in American homes.

SANTA SPEAKING

The tradition of a military Santa Tracker began with a Sears ad that published Santa's phone number. Trouble was, one child dialed wrong and ended up on the phone with the officer on duty at the Continental Air Defense Command (CONAD, predecessor to the North American Aerospace Defense Command, or NORAD). The officer played along and reported the progress of Santa's sleigh, which has become an enduring Christmas Eve practice.

TOP SHELF MAGAZINE

Richard Sears was competing with the established Montgomery Ward catalog, and knew customers held on to their catalogs. He made his a little bit smaller so it would stack neatly on top of the competition.

YOUR HOLIDAY IS IN THE MAIL

Turn-of-the-century catalogs sold Christmas items such as ornaments, cards and wax candles for trees. As its customers grew safety-minded, the catalog offered artificial trees and electric tree lights. Shoppers began to think of the catalog as a source for holiday gifts, and the first just-for-Christmas catalog came out in 1933.

WASTE NOT

Outdated Sears catalogs enjoyed a second life in America's privies. The company supposedly received many complaints from its outhouse-owning customers when it began to print colored pictures on coated paper stock.

FAMOUS FACES

Lauren Bacall, Susan Hayward and Gloria Swanson all modeled for Sears. Roy Rogers, Ted Williams and Gene Autry also popped up on its pages.

THAT WAS ONE BUSY ELF

Our mom, Jane, always wanted us to have the best Christmas that she and our dad, Donald, could afford, and she made sure it was perfect.

We'd pore over the pages of the Sears wish book, then tell her what we wanted from Santa. She worked tirelessly to keep everything a secret. We learned years later that Mom charged all those orders on her revolving charge account and spent the whole year paying them off.

Donna Dugger Depeyster • DeLand, FL

Living in town, I had a sidewalk to skate on, so when the Sears wish book came, I immediately turned to the roller skates. They were just what I needed: There was a key I could use to secure them and they even had ball bearings. To my delight, there they were under the tree on Christmas Day.

Kay Schluessler • Edwardsport, IN

It had pages and pages of the necessities and luxuries of life. But to my foreign service family living in Madras, India, in the 1950s, it was our connection to all things American—and our window to our homeland.

Michele Ivy Davis • Escondido, CA

My oldest brother was a grade school teacher and principal, and he has a very good imagination. When his children were growing up, he read the Sears wish book like a story to his children.

Sue Halldorsson • Fort Wayne, IN

Whenever Mom needed some quiet time, she would give my brother Lon and me each a crayon and tell us to mark what we wanted Santa to bring us. By the week before Christmas you couldn't even read the pages with the Tonka trucks on them.

Jay Chester • Fort Myers, FL

SISTERS IN HARMONY

Girls gave Uncle Bill a sweet earful at Christmas.

Davison
sisters
Wendy,
Deborah,
Rita and Jean
(in front)
had natural
musical
talent.

Our father, a self-taught tenor sax player and a popular bandleader in the Big Band era before he shipped out to the Pacific theater in World War II, taught us girls to sing in harmony. I was the oldest, and using my babysitting money, I bought sheet music at Polsky's department store in downtown Akron, Ohio. None of us could read music, but I figured out our harmonies on an old player piano.

The Lennon Sisters on *The Lawrence Welk Show*—like us, four girls—were an influence. Wendy sang the melody, I sang alto, Rita sang third-part harmony and our baby sister, Jean, called Goody, punctuated our songs with ho-ho-hos or whatever else we needed.

When we were on our way to visit our relatives and get our Christmas loot—we were poor, so this was a big deal—we warmed up our voices by singing in the car. Our wealthy Scottish uncle, Bill, always encouraged us to sing, and rewarded us with loud applause and a shouted "Encore! Encore!" When I was 15 or so, around 1961, our Aunt Ethel arranged for us to sing at the Fairlawn Country Club Christmas party. She even bought us matching red jumpers with white blouses for the occasion.

We were such a hit that the veterans club invited us to sing on its radio broadcast in Uniontown. Our repertoire included "Silent Night," "Winter Wonderland," "Jingle Bells" and many more favorite Christmas songs.

Deborah Whitford • Phoenix, AZ

Gary and Sandra earned money by helping their grandparents.

EARNING AN HONEST DIME

Chore by chore, the Christmas jar filled up.

Growing up in San Jacinto, California, in the mid-1950s, my brothers and I were fortunate to live near both sets of our grandparents. My older brother, Gary, earned money helping my grandpa who lived down the street with yardwork. I spent most of my time with my Grandma Livesay, who lived next door. She was short on money, but long on time and fun: She taught me how to knit, crochet and make pie.

One day at Grandma Livesay's, I was moping that Gary had money and I didn't. The next day, there was an empty jar on her table. Grandma told me that if I'd sweep the front porch, she'd put a whole dime in that jar for me. I was small and the broom was big, but that didn't stop me. I was on my way to being rich!

I dried dishes, dusted, folded towels— no job was too small, and they all paid a nickel or dime. My brother might have a paper bill with a 5 on it, but my jar was filling with coins.

At Christmastime, we counted the money. One special day, Grandma and I walked to Sherwood's, a five-and-dime in downtown San Jacinto. With gentle reminders from Grandma that I couldn't spend more than what was jingling in my pocket, I carefully picked out a scarf for Mom, a handkerchief for Dad and small toys for my two brothers.

No presents were ever more lovingly wrapped, and I put them under the tree with pride, knowing I'd earned the money for each one. Those gifts gave me more joy than any I received that year.

I realize now that my grandparents had very little money, and so it was with great sacrifice and love that Grandma put those nickels and dimes in that jar.

Sandra Packham • Monroe, WA

Jesse and Joanna were lucky to experience a downtown Minneapolis tradition.

CHRISTMAS PILGRIMAGE TO THE CITIES

Fantasy came to life on department store's eighth floor.

My sister Joanna, my friend Rachael and I belted out the lyrics from the backseat of the minivan. "FIVE GO-O-OLD RINGS!"

In the front, Mom and Dad smiled at our spirited rendition of the Christmas song as we sped toward Minneapolis-St. Paul after school.

We lived about an hour north, and going to "the cities," as we called them, was always a big deal. One afternoon each Christmas season, we made the trip to enjoy the store window displays and the magical eighth-floor wonderland at Dayton's downtown Minneapolis department store, where a different story was portrayed every year.

Exiting the elevator, we were immersed in a sparkling world filled with music. We followed a path through the maze of animatronic characters set up to tell a well-known story, such as *Pinocchio* or *The Wizard of Oz*. There were always candy canes and cookies for the kids.

When we reached the end, we'd get back in line and walk through the scene again, trying to spot things we missed the first time. Thinking back on it, I'm amazed at how much work must have gone into creating these productions each year.

The days of Dayton's eighth-floor display are long gone, but luckily for my sister and me—and likely many others—the magic of the cities at Christmastime lives on in our memories.

Jesse Neve • *Minnetrista, MN*

The Man Behind the Suit

My parents owned a dry-cleaning shop in Lafayette, Louisiana. Every year, an important client brought his red suit to the shop for cleaning.

In 1948, when I was 2, I knew the man with the special outfit and the smiling eyes as Santa. My mom, Evala Cormier, knew him as Jeff, and she became friends with him through taking care of that annual assignment.

In December 1971, Mom—then a grandma—and I took my son Heath to visit Santa at the mall in Lafayette. Mom was surprised to recognize the man in red: It was Jeff, still spreading Christmas cheer after all those years. He was so happy to meet my son.

It still touches my heart to think of our unlikely reunion with this kind man.

Elaine C. Bourgeois • Slidell, LA

Santa remembered Elaine and her mom, Evala, below, when he met Heath, left, in 1971.

SANTA VISITS

The very first department store Santa Claus is believed to have been James "Colonel Jim" Edgar of Brockton, Massachusetts.

Edgar, who owned a dry goods store, liked dressing up to surprise shoppers. In the weeks before Christmas in 1890, he appeared in his store wearing a custom Santa suit.

Meeting a real Santa was a dream come true for kids, who came from other cities to visit with him.

The following year, many stores got their own Santas. By the turn of the 20th century, the annual visit to the department store to tell Santa what you wanted was a Christmas tradition.

A GUST OF SEASONAL SPIRIT

Baby, it was cold outside—and inside.

Christmas 1965 was bitterly cold in southwest Ohio. For several days prior to the holiday, winds were high, especially at night, creating snow drifts and wreaking havoc with exterior decorations. Plastic reindeer and nativity wise men were strewn onto snowbanks, and strings of colored lights drooped from roof gutters. I rode to morning kindergarten in a warm station wagon with several other 5-year-olds, but my poor sister Mischelle and the other older kids had to trudge through the elements to school.

But however rough the weather, it was still the Christmas season, and an exciting time for everyone. My sister and I had already circled several items in the Sears wish book. With five years separating us, our choices seldom overlapped. But that year, we both asked for a Heidi pocketbook doll. She wore a cute little dress, and when you pressed her tummy her right hand flew up as if to say "Hi."

For weeks, Mischelle and I perked up every time we heard the "Hi, Heidi" commercial jingle on TV. Stormy weather or not, we were sure Santa would deliver the goods, and our thumbs were poised to press those Heidi tummy buttons.

ANA HARD

Christmas Eve night was particularly windy, but it was cozy inside our house. I tried hard to stay awake, but I fell asleep watching my grandmother assemble the fruit salad she always made at Christmas. Someone carried me to the double bed that I shared with Mischelle, and she joined me there not long afterward. The grown-ups had far too much to do to go to bed early. Grandmother was busy in the kitchen. My mother wrapped gifts while my father assembled toys until after midnight.

I don't know how Mischelle and I slept through it, but sometime in the wee hours of Christmas morning, the fierce wind blew out the window in our front room. Glass flew everywhere. The Christmas tree blew over, ornaments shattered and presents were torn and crushed. The house filled with frigid air.

It must have been an ordeal for the adults to deal with. All I know is that when Mischelle and I ran down the hall at around 7 that morning to see what Santa had brought us, we found layers of cardboard pressed against the hole in the window, held in place by the nose of the ironing board, which was upside down on the sofa. All four chairs of our kitchen dining set were on top of the couch, holding the ironing board in place.

Torn wrapping paper had been hurriedly patched with a mix of tape and Christmas seals. And it was quite chilly in that room.

We looked around in disbelief as three exhausted adults ambled in. They tried to explain what happened, but Mischelle and I rushed to the presents. Within minutes, we were happily waving at each other with our Heidi dolls. Christmas is still Christmas, after all.

Later, as we stood around the kitchen table eating fruit salad, wearing our winter coats over our pajamas, we laughed at the ridiculous situation. We knew that we would laugh about it for many Christmases to come—and we did, just as I'm laughing now, more than 50 years later.

Marla Cross • *New Carlisle, OH*

TONKA TRUCK CHRISTMAS

Santa proved he could read between the lines.

O n the Saturday after Thanksgiving, over giant bowls of Lucky Charms, my sister Staci and I studied the Sears Christmas wish book. A 3-inch tome often used as a booster seat at the dinner table, the pages were stuffed with dreams for two curious farm girls in the mid-1960s. We took our Christmas lists seriously. Santa had to see us through to summer birthdays.

After crafting my letter to the North Pole, I proofread my little sister's. At the top of her list was "Tonka Truck."

"No! That's a boy's present," I told her. Although we both had tomboy tendencies, favoring tree climbing over tea parties, I couldn't allow her to waste her main gift on a boy's present. Our grandfather Papa Creecy would buy us boy presents at the mere mention of a Matchbox car or a baseball bat.

She erased and erased and erased until she almost ripped the notepaper. With help from our mother, Barbara, she wrote "Barbie car" over the worn spot. Then we taped our letters near the fireplace in the living room.

I stared at my sister's letter. With all that erasing, it was messy and wrinkled.

"Maybe you should write your list over," I suggested.

"Don't worry, it's fine," Momma said.

"It's fine," Staci repeated. She stuck her tongue out at me when Momma wasn't looking.

Snow fell during the night and we woke to a rare white Christmas. Still, I was anxious—had we been good enough? Fearing a cold living room empty of presents on Christmas morning, I sent Staci ahead to scout.

She tiptoed off in her footie pajamas while I pulled the bedspread to my chin and waited. The house was silent except for the hum of the wall furnace.

"He came!" she whispered, her eyes grown wide.

I exhaled, relieved. The simple fact that Santa managed to locate our farmhouse chimney year after year was amazing to me. I partially attributed this continued good fortune to our daily consumption of Lucky Charms.

"What did he bring?" I asked, throwing back the covers.

"Lots of stuff. I just looked from the door, so it would be a surprise."

We saw stacks of books, two board games and new Barbie outfits. And something else.

We stared dumbstruck at the Christmas miracle parked underneath the Scotch pine. Even though she had erased it from the list, Santa knew exactly what Staci really wanted after all.

Talya Tate Boerner • Dallas, TX

SWEET RIDE

Her dream finally came true.

My sister had a way with words—but not the ones I wanted to hear. "Listen, you brat," she said one year, "what makes you think you're getting a bike for Christmas?"

My yearning for a bicycle of my own had taken over my young life. It seemed that each birthday and Christmas, I was having a harder time hiding my disappointment. I didn't want dolls, clothes or toys, only my two-wheeled dream.

As my eighth birthday approached, my parents explained that because a bike wasn't in their budget that year, they were giving me a day at The Pike amusement park in Long Beach—just Mom, Dad and me. I was one of six children, so this was indeed a treat.

My parents sat through two movies of my choice—a Western with Johnny Mack Brown and a Tarzan flick with Johnny Weissmuller—and bought me my first cotton candy. It was a magical day.

Still, it wasn't a bike.

The Christmas after I turned 9, I was beginning to despair that I'd ever have a two-wheeler to call my own. The family was opening gifts, and I could see that nothing was big enough to suggest "bike" under all the wrapped presents.

Then my father said, "Patty, would you please bring me some handkerchiefs from the bedroom?"

I did as requested, but when I opened the door, my eyes popped.

There sat a yellow balloon-tired girl's bicycle, with the word "ROCKET" down the front fork in bright blue letters. I ran back to my dad.

"There's a bike in there!" The whole family cheered.

I have received many wonderful gifts over the years, but nothing matched the shiny yellow beauty I got the Christmas of my ninth year.

Patricia Edwards • *Fullerton, CA*

LASTING DREAM CAPTURED IN A TENDER TRAP

Desire is an engine that smokes and whistles.

Back in 1958, I'd pore through the Lionel toy train catalog and drool over the Norfolk and Western 746 Class J Northern steam locomotive. I'd never seen anything so magnificent. The smooth bullet-nose engine with its orange and yellow stripe and sleek streamlined black tender (coal car) captivated me.

Together the engine and tender measured a little shy of 2 feet—enormous by the toy train standards of the day. Even better, the 746 had a working headlight and smoker, and its tender whistled.

Unfortunately, the magnificent 746 also had a magnificent price—$50, or the equivalent of about $450 today.

That was far more than my mother could afford. Instead, I had to be content with my grandfather's little Lionel plastic engine and tender, which was 6 inches shorter than the 746 and had no headlight, smoker or whistle.

Years passed, but my interest in toy trains never waned, nor did my admiration for the Lionel 746, which continued to appreciate in value. When I was in my 30s, a 746 could sell for $1,000 or more.

When I retired in 1997, sophisticated sound systems and computer controls dominated hobby trains. Though I still admired the 746 at train shows, I spent my money elsewhere.

In the last few years, however, my old interest in postwar trains returned, and I began to search for a 746. A good one was still commanding a princely price of around $1,000. But in time I stumbled on a 746 in excellent condition on an internet auction site. It was listed at less than half the usual asking price.

I bid and held my breath, certain that a bevy of last-minute bids would take the toy out of my range. That never happened. My win was a fluke, helped, I believe, by an error in the listing, which had buried the 746 in with modern-era trains instead of in the postwar category where it belonged.

It is fitting that my 746 arrived in time for Christmas. I immediately placed it under the tree, turned off all the lights except for the Christmas lights, and let the venerable legend strut its stuff. Smoke billowed from the engine and the soft whistle sounded from its tender.

For a brief moment time stood still. I was both 11 and 67—the dream of my youth had finally come true.

Michael D. Hayward • *Clementon, NJ*

Santa in Palm Land

When ho-ho-ho turns hot-hot-hot.

ALL IS BRIGHT

Florida Memory, the state library and archives of Florida, has a trove of pictures from individuals and companies gathered over the decades. These are among the dozens of holiday-themed images at *floridamemory.com*.

1: *Santa Claus waves from the midst of a crowd gathered at a pier in St. Augustine in a state Department of Commerce promotional photo taken in 1951.*
2: *Noted commercial photographer Joseph Janney Steinmetz took this 1965 shot of Santa picking oranges in Sarasota.*
3: *Another shot from Steinmetz's 1965 series—this showing Santa as he navigates a Sarasota canal.*
4: *The City News Bureau of St. Petersburg snapped a barefoot Santa and friends going over the naughty-and-nice list in this undated photo.*

Unforgettable Holiday Chestnut

A classic Christmas tune glows with Yuletide cheer.

By Mary-Liz Shaw

Many people call it by its first line, "Chestnuts roasting on an open fire"—not surprising, considering its actual title, "The Christmas Song," sounds oddly generic, as if the songwriters always meant to come up with something better. Yet this seasonal favorite, composed on a blistering hot July day by Mel Tormé and Robert Wells and first recorded by Nat King Cole in 1946, may be the most finely crafted tune in the holiday canon.

Tormé's haunting jazz melody aligns perfectly with its lyrical storytelling, which is a tribute to all the special moments that "help to make the season bright": Jack Frost nipping at your nose, Yuletide carols being sung by a choir, and a turkey and some mistletoe.

The song's most unusual feature is its structure: It has no chorus. Instead, it builds with a progressive chord sequence to the final "simple phrase" of "Merry Christmas to you."

And completing the masterwork is Cole's incomparable voice, warm as an embrace.

If you aren't humming "The Christmas Song" by now, perhaps these musical notes about it will help you along.

SPEED WRITING

Tormé (right) went to Wells' home in Toluca Lake, California, on one of the hottest days of 1945 and saw what soon became the first verse of "The Christmas Song" scribbled on a notepad. Wells said the heat was so oppressive that he thought he might cool off by writing about a chilly winter's day. Tormé tried a few notes on the piano and they had their new song in about 45 minutes.

LET'S ASK NAT!

As Mel's son James told National Public Radio in 2017, the duo knew that their holiday tune was something special. They took it to a music publisher, where they got a big, fat no. Nobody would want a song that could only be played at Christmas, the publisher explained. Undeterred, Tormé and Wells went to Nat King Cole, who was playing at the Trocadero nightclub in Los Angeles.

"I told him (Tormé) it was beautiful," Cole told jazz writer Leonard Feather in 1961. "But I didn't feel it would be right to do it with just a trio."

MANY TIMES, MANY WAYS

Despite his reservations about recording "The Christmas Song" with only his King Cole Trio, Cole did just that at a New York studio in June 1946. Two months later he persuaded Capitol Records to let him try again, this time with a light string arrangement over the jazz trio.

Cole went on to record two more versions, in 1953 and 1961, each time with even more strings. Cole's first 1946 version was inducted into the Grammy Hall of Fame, but it's his 1961 recording that most people know.

It is one of the most recorded Christmas hits of all time, with treatments by artists such as Ella Fitzgerald, George Strait, Christina Aguilera and Michael Buble. A very popular version is from Frank Sinatra, who sang it on his first Christmas LP in 1957 (above).

WHY NOT MEL?

Though less well known than Cole at the time, Tormé was himself an accomplished jazz performer with a silver-toned voice. Some have wondered why he didn't record "The Christmas Song" first.

"Nat Cole was simply exploding at that particular moment in time," James Tormé told NPR. It made more sense for Cole to run with it.

MULTITASKER

A child prodigy in music, Tormé wrote his first hit, "Lament for Love" (for Harry James' orchestra, no less) at age 15. He also was an expert drummer, pianist and arranger. In his later years, he took up writing, penning a well-regarded book about Judy Garland, *The Other Side of the Rainbow*, and his autobiography, *It Wasn't All Velvet*—a reference to his nickname, the Velvet Fog, which he never liked.

THE GIFT THAT KEEPS GIVING

Though occasionally befuddled by the wild popularity of his most famous composition—written when he was just 19—Tormé enjoyed its returns. He wrote that Cole's recording of "The Christmas Song" resulted in his "financial pleasure" and once joked that the tune was "my annuity."

Tormé wrote at least one other holiday song, "The Christmas Feeling." His son James, also a jazz singer, now performs it.

Nat King Cole sings as Mel Tormé plays piano with King Cole Trio members Irving Ashby and Johnny Miller on bass, c. 1945.

ONE-HORSE OPEN SLEIGH

Banker had extra duties at Christmas.

My father, Laurence Chabot, worked at the First National Bank in Ontonagon, Michigan—first as cashier and later as president. For several years, as part of our small-town Christmas, he had local artisans carve an ice horse in front of the bank. Of course, Dad couldn't resist doing a little shaving himself.

The horse was complete with real reins, a sleigh and a lap robe, and many people in our Upper Michigan town posed for pictures with it. Several of Dad's friends had their own tradition of dumping fresh manure under the horse, which brought big laughs.

We five kids had jobs at Christmas, too. The decorations were kept in our attic, which we reached with a pull-down ladder. Our mom, Mae, stored her cardboard fireplace there, along with her altar-boy candles. To retrieve things, we had to balance our way across the joists to avoid crashing through the floor to a bedroom below.

I tended our balky furnace, and as I stoked it each night during World War II, I could have sworn there was an enemy machine-gun nest in the coal bin and Nazis in the fruit cellar.

As the second oldest, I felt superior knowing Dad's secret: On Christmas Eve, he put a hay bale for Santa's reindeer next to the side door. Then he sneaked up the street with a set of sleigh bells. We kids listened for the bells, and when they got close, Mom shooed us upstairs before Santa caught us out of bed. In the morning, all of us hunted for the bale, but the hay was mostly gone and the snow under it was trampled—proof that Santa had been there.

As we grew older, we joined our parents at midnight Mass and then went home to bed while they attended a party. After the party, all the dads headed downtown, where the store owners waited with Christmas orders to be picked up. The wee hours were spent assembling and wrapping presents. No wonder Dad dozed in a chair while we opened our presents.

After Christmas, the decorations had to be returned to the attic. We again tiptoed over the joists, putting everything away until next year.

Larry Chabot • Marquette, MI

A VIVID PINK SANTA

She happily kept the jolly decoration all these years.

Annette's son, Stevie, poses with the rosy-cheeked Santa on Christmas Day 1970.

n 1962, I was 23 years old, teaching school and living with my parents in Niles, Ohio.

An avid shopper, I loved spending my weekends browsing through stores in hopes of finding remarkable deals.

I spent most Saturdays in Youngstown, Ohio, a bustling city during pre-mall days. You could find high-end merchandise at Livingston's and McKelvey's, while Lustig's and Baker's shoe stores met all foot needs. There was also a millinery shop in the Bus Arcade that attracted a large flock of customers. I combed the less-expensive bargain stores as well as upscale businesses.

One Saturday, in Youngstown's Central Square, I followed my instincts and found myself in the right store at the right time. The right store was Murphy's five-and-dime; the right time, mid-December.

Inside Murphy's, Christmas merchandise was whimsical, plentiful and reasonably priced. My eyes immediately landed on a fashionable decorative Santa Claus. He stood 15 inches high and wore a pink velvet suit trimmed with soft white fur. Boots and a belt, both shiny white, further enhanced his outfit. I purchased the burly, white-bearded, crimson-faced

replica with good reason: My bedroom, many of my favorite clothes, and my personal Emerson radio were all pink! How could I pass up this remarkable treasure when pink was all the rage?

When my husband and I married in 1965, we packed up the pink Santa with my belongings and moved him to our new apartment in Niles. Four years later, after our son was born, the three of us settled in Brookfield, Ohio; once again, Mr. Claus relocated with us. The tile in our kitchen was pink, and we reupholstered the chairs in pink leather. At Christmastime, Santa occupied the top of a tea cart, perfectly complementing our eating area.

We remodeled our kitchen in 1990. As country green was in and pink was out, I permanently retired my beloved possession.

Today the carefully wrapped Saint Nick sits on the top shelf of a hall closet. Every year, as I unpack the Christmas decorations, I routinely unwrap and admire my rare treasure. In original, perfect form, my nostalgic, vivid Santa continues to charm his beholder.

Annette Kochera • Brookfield, OH

THE FABRIC OF LOVE

One lean Yuletide, a family gained unexpected riches.

When the big box arrived that year, my brother Randy, my sister Linda and I were in school. Gary and Mark, still preschoolers, watched as Mom opened the parcel of fabric remnants from her old friend Mrs. Spritke, who worked at Rhea Manufacturing Co. garment factory in Milwaukee, Wisconsin. Mom told the boys that the package was a secret. They were to tell no one about it.

Nearly a year had passed since Dad's bowling pin refinishing shop had burned down in early December 1954. His efforts to re-establish the business hadn't worked out, so Christmas 1955 was going to be meager in the Anderson household.

We'd moved from Milwaukee to rural Osseo, Wisconsin, where Mom had roots, and were living in a rented farmhouse. That summer, Mom and Dad both worked in our big garden every chance they could. Dad quipped, "We'll eat what we can. What we can't, we'll can."

Dad and I cut wood with a two-man saw to feed the furnace and the kitchen's Monarch range. On weekends, I hunted rabbits and squirrels.

We were nearly self-sufficient, but we all knew that few if any of our Christmas wishes would come true that season.

"I sure would like a record player for Christmas," Randy said.

Then Linda added her wish. "It would be so neat to have a new winter coat."

I dreamed of a red-and-black plaid hunting jacket. And so it went, each of us hoping for something out of reach.

For weeks before Christmas, Mom holed up in the spare bedroom working on secret projects. It was obvious she was sewing—the floor vibrated as her old Singer rumbled through its paces.

"You'd think that thing would take off soon, the way she revs it up," Dad joked.

Dad confided in me that he'd sold some of his tools and sporting equipment and used the money to buy a new dress for Mom, and a secondhand trike and wagon for Gary and Mark. For several nights, I helped Dad sand and repaint the toys. The others had their secret projects, too, but woe to any snoops.

About a week before the holiday, Dad and I cut a tree from the woods and we all trimmed it with the decorations that had survived the move from the city, adding a few new homemade adornments.

It felt miraculous that on Christmas Eve we had a stack of presents under the tree. Most were wrapped in newspaper, but they looked beautiful. After dinner, we gathered in the living room to sing carols, read a Christmas story and open our gifts.

By doing odd jobs, Dad had managed to scrape enough together to get each of us a store-bought present. I still have the pocketknife he gave me that night.

All of the kids made presents for each other and our parents. One of the most creative was the cardboard replica record player—complete with an arm that moved and a rotating turntable—that Gary made for Randy.

Then we opened our gifts from Mom. They were more than works of art. They were acts of love. Linda's winter coat looked professionally tailored. Dad and Randy wore their wool shirts for years. The matching bib overalls for Mark and Gary were perfect. And for me? A red-and-black plaid hunting coat.

We never forgot that special Christmas, 1955—the year of our material wealth.

Glenn Anderson • Spooner, WI

Do You Hear What I Hear?

The radio wasn't on much in the house when I was a little guy—I was born in 1946—but one show I remember hearing was *The Cinnamon Bear*. In Chicago, the children's adventure written by Glanville and Elisabeth Heisch aired on WGN in 15-minute episodes on weekdays between Thanksgiving and Christmas.

I loved listening to those episodes, which ended on a cliffhanger each night. The story begins with siblings Jimmy and Judy searching the attic for their family's missing Christmas tree star. A toy bear comes to life to tell them the Crazy Quilt Dragon stole it. The bear transports the brother and sister to Maybeland to get back the star.

In the 1970s, when our daughter was 5 years old, I splurged on a set of cassettes of the series so she could enjoy the story as I had. She played those tapes year after year. By the time her twin boys were born, the tapes had worn out and a few were missing, but we found a new version on compact disc.

Three generations of our family have thrilled to the adventures of Paddy O'Cinnamon. And his tale lives on. It's available on the internet now.

What a gift that is for children—to hear a story as their imagination fills in the pictures. Even as an adult, I still enjoy listening to an old radio show at bedtime.

Richard Ploch • Waynesville, NC

Pictures from the Past

CHRISTMAS DAY

TINSEL TIME

My brother Arthur and his new puppy watch our mom, Natalie, decorate the tree in our home in Framingham, Massachusetts, in 1966. I don't remember the puppy's name, because we quickly learned that Arthur was allergic, and we had to find it a new home.

Joan Hileman • *Lynchburg, VA*

SIMPLE GIFTS

At 3 months old, my brother Michael is content between myself, 9, and Tunde, 13, for his first Christmas in 1994. For me, this photo my mother took many years ago at the family home in Nigeria marks a turning point in my rivalry with my older brother. Mother bought me a dress with Christmas colors so I would feel special. She asked me to smile, but I couldn't overlook the fact that Tunde had finally won and now had a partner in crime (Michael) who would soon terrorize my dolls.

Esther Samson Ukaria
Mülheim an der Ruhr, Germany

WARM THOUGHTS

I took this snapshot of my wife, Gladys, and my mother, Ueber, opening gifts on Christmas Day while soaking up the sun at Lake Seminole Resort in Largo, Florida, in 1957.

Donald Marks

PLACE OF HONOR

Every Christmas, members of the Heffner family took a moment to pose in front of the fireplace. It was my mother's favorite feature of the house my parents built in 1957. The lovely stone fireplace would prove to be the background for many special holidays.

Gail Heffner-Charles • Lithopolis, OH

CRISP MEMORIES

Surprise find was a present from the past.

A Christmas memory that warms my heart is the sweet taste of my mother's spritz cookies made with an old-time aluminum Mirro cookie press that she inherited from her mother.

Throughout the year, Mom was usually too busy to bake; she took care of five kids and had a job at the shirt factory. But every Christmas, without fail, she produced these tiny tree cookies that seemed miraculous to me as a young child. They weren't perfect, but they symbolized a busy woman's love during an even busier time of year.

Mom's cookie press eventually became mine, and I was delighted to carry on the tradition of spritz cookies at holiday time.

Until one December day, when the press broke right in the middle of my cookie baking. The handle came loose and fell off. Those many decades of cookie production finally took their toll on the antique press handed down from Mom's mom.

Disappointed and upset, I searched for a replacement, but new presses just weren't the same as the old one that I loved.

Sometime later, my Dad's sister passed away. She lived alone in her parents' old house, so afterward, I helped Dad clean out the place.

We found many treasures, but to this day I still can't believe what I came across in a dusty corner of the cellar—a 1935 Mirro cookie press. It was still in its original box, with a recipe booklet and all the discs standing neatly in the rack. It was as if it had been waiting for me to find it.

That was years ago, and ever since I have been using that cookie press—this one inherited from Dad's mom—to make my spritz trees at Christmas.

Here's hoping someday I can pass the press on to my new granddaughter. And I'll be sure to tell her the story behind it, just as I recount it to family members each holiday season.

Anita Gogno • Hatfield, PA

LEFT: TASTE OF HOME

SAVORING A SWEET FRIENDSHIP

*Peg and Esther's baking sessions
were a highlight of the holiday season.*

My parents, Peg and Earl Waggett, and I, then 5, moved from Pennsylvania to Akron, Ohio, in 1945. Within a few days, we visited what became our new church, and the first person we met was Esther Fox, who warmly welcomed us. So began Mom and Esther's friendship, a blessing to my stay-at-home mother, who knew few people in our new community.

Esther and Mom started a tradition of spending a full day during the holiday season making cookies. When I got home from school, I mixed icing for the freshly baked treats.

Surrounded by candies and colored sugar, I joyously decorated cutout Santas, Christmas trees, angels and stars until they were just right—and I occasionally snacked on one or two that weren't.

After Dad died in 1973, Mom returned to Pennsylvania, but she kept up her friendship with Esther. Mom died in 2011. The next year, Esther, then 94, sent me a Christmas box of commercially prepared cookies, a touching and thoughtful gift. Then, in 2013, she sent me homemade sugar cookies with tubes of frosting. Decorating them, I savored memories of doing the same thing at the gray Formica table in Ohio all those years ago. I recalled a notation my mother had written next to Esther's name in our address book: "A girl's best friend."

I still have the cookie cutters Mom and Esther used during their baking sessions. At Esther's 100th birthday party in 2018, I drove from central Kentucky to Akron for the celebration, bringing with me decorated cookies in the shapes of hearts, stars and angels.

Sandra Waggett Miller • Lexington, KY

Sandra posed with her parents, Peg and Earl Waggett, above. Peg later made a lifelong friend of Esther, right.

Season of Giving

Soldiers brought the Christmas spirit to refugees in Belgium.

My holidays were always filled with family and friends, over-decorated trees with many gifts under their branches and an abundance of food. But I never knew what Christmas was really about until 1944, in Belgium.

My Army unit had moved through biting winds and snow into an area of doubtful alliances (it was a former SS resort). We scrounged around for anything to make us more comfortable—blankets, bedsprings, stoves, you name it. Me? I found a box of Christmas ornaments and stowed them on the Army truck.

On Dec. 16, the Battle of the Bulge intervened and kept us moving in and out of action, obliterating all thoughts of the holiday. But by Christmas Eve, we stopped at a refugee camp that sheltered hundreds of mothers and children—all very sad and very hungry.

My lights suddenly went on. *This is the reason you kept those Christmas ornaments,* I thought. *Now find a tree.*

I approached a friendly sergeant with my idea. He was all for it, so we jumped into a jeep and drove until we spotted our tree. Back at the camp, the sergeant and I suggested that each man in our company contribute a sock full of rations for the refugees. Word quickly passed through all the companies, and everybody gave.

The next day, the tree was up and fully decorated. We invited folks from the refugee camp, and they walked into a celebration they never would have imagined. Our guests looked at the tree in amazement. The branches were laden with found ornaments, packs of cigarettes, chewing gum and radar tinsel.

We handed each kid a full Army sock, which reached to the floor. The youngest

3

children clung to their mothers or bigger siblings. They seemed a bit overwhelmed, but the older kids enjoyed themselves. Some of the soldiers played carols on guitars while others sang. We talked to the refugees with the help of some of our bilingual soldiers.

The U.S. Army feeds its troops well, and our Christmas dinner was no exception. We wanted to give our meals to the refugee mothers, but it wasn't allowed. All leftovers had to be thrown out. Starving mothers waited to pull the discarded food from the trash. I knew from the grins on my buddies' faces that those mothers rescued hundreds of complete dinners that day.

I'll never forget that Christmas, when all of us soldiers truly gave from our hearts.

John Jarvie • Kearny, NJ

1, 5: *Cpl. John Jarvie put his artistic skills to use photographing and sketching kids he encountered at a refugee camp in 1944.*
2-4: *John (2) learned the meaning of Christmas during World War II, when his Army unit hosted a holiday celebration for hungry refugees, including hundreds of children (3, 4).*

LIGHT UP
THE JUNGLE

*An unexpected delivery brought holiday cheer
to plenty of young men.*

Our brother, Sgt. David Erhardt, was stationed at Cam Ranh Bay Air Base in South Vietnam in 1966. Periodically, we sent him care packages that included envelopes of Kool-Aid to add to the potable water to disguise the chemical compounds added for purification. We also sent cookies, but they were often reduced to crumbs by the time they reached their destination. Yet even the crumbs were scooped up and enjoyed.

In late November, we all wanted to send David something that would spell "home" in capital letters. One of our most important family Christmas rituals started with gathering around the tree and singing "O Tannenbaum." So we decided to send him a Christmas tree. A tall order maybe, but not for us. Where there was a will, there was a way.

We commandeered a tree from the company office: a fully decorated artificial tabletop fir. Glass ornaments, colored lights and strands of tinsel hung from its branches. An angel sat on top. We didn't know if the lights could be used, but the men could imagine the tree all lit up. After all, what was Christmas without lights?

We were unaware that a generator was set up outside David's "hoochie," which in his case was a tent-topped screened cabin. (Outside hung a sign that read "Another McDonald's coming soon.")

We carefully wrapped the package in heavy brown paper, thick twine, and yards and yards of tape. After a trip to the post office, the tree was on its way.

When mail call came and David got his package, he was expecting scads of cookies. Imagine his surprise when he opened it

Christmas in Vietnam, Dec. 22, 1966, a U.S. soldier reads a card while sitting on supplies with a festive tree in the background.

and found a tree, completely intact, fully decorated and waiting to be plugged in. The switch was flipped and the hoochie was filled with twinkling lights.

Now, decades later, we still talk about the wonder of that special surprise Christmas tree.

Nancy Macisco • *Trumbull, CT*

Gene Lowry, one of Hal's buddies, gets a box from Santa.

CHRISTMAS IN THE BARRACKS

Homesick airmen made the best of it.

During the latter part of the Korean War, I was an aircraft mechanic assigned to a flight line maintenance squadron at Nellis Air Force Base near Las Vegas, Nevada. We maintained the F-86 Sabres used for training fighter pilots.

We were low-ranking—and low-paid—servicemen. The joke was that a three-stripe airman first class got $117 per day—once a month. For a two-stripe airman second class, the rate was $101.40.

Over the holidays, the flying schedule was reduced to allow as many of us as possible to get home. Part of the unit got leave for Christmas, the other part for New Year's. For those guys who couldn't get leave for Christmas 1956, there was no Bing Crosby and no snow—just homesickness and a lack of privacy in our open bay barracks.

We celebrated with a tree we found on the side of the highway. Its snowy decoration, and the fake beard one of the guys applied, came from a shaving kit. Broke as we were, our buffet was Christmas-package leftovers, and the dress code for the occasion was off-duty casual. But I recall that the mess hall meal was outstanding: turkey with all the side dishes.

Our outfit had a Christmas tradition that the officers worked on the serving line that day—a practice that was still going on when I retired from the service 28 years later. Those memories we created get better with each passing year.

Hal Fulton • Wooster, OH

FOR AGGIE

An epic journey to see the woman he couldn't forget.

Now a widower, I am blessed with many memories. But the one that stands out the most in my mind is of Christmas Eve 1954. It was about 8 p.m. and a heavy snow was falling when I finally arrived at my destination, a small farmhouse by a creek near the town of McArthur in the hill country of southeastern Ohio.

I had hitchhiked 525 miles to visit a very special girl by the name of Agnes "Aggie" Johnson.

I'd left Norfolk, Virginia, the evening before to see her one last time before my ship, the USS *Midway*, left for duty in the South China Sea.

I have a vivid memory of the sound of my own feet running across the old wooden bridge over the creek. Christmas lights twinkled in the windows and reflected off the deep snow. Agnes heard me and rushed out to greet me.

ANA HARD

Inside, Agnes and I visited with her parents for a while, then we exchanged gifts. We talked in that way young people do, enjoying each other's company. It was a beautiful, chilly winter wonderland outside, while inside it was warm as toast by the wood and coal fire.

The next morning—Christmas Day—I left at 7 to hitchhike back to Norfolk and to my ship, which was set to leave port at 6 a.m. on the 27th.

On the way back, I got snowed in for nearly a whole day in the mountain town of East Rainelle, West Virginia. Fortunately, I was able to flag a Greyhound bus that was plowing its way through the drifts, which took me to the bus depot in Norfolk.

I managed to make it aboard the Midway very early on Dec. 27, with barely three hours to spare before we shipped out.

The next year, Agnes and I married. The memories of that Christmas Eve, especially, are etched into my very being. I call on them often to warm my heart, and to remind myself of what this life is all about.

If life is not about love and giving, I don't know what it is. There is nothing so precious as the love we receive and the love we give to others.

John Louis Kokalis • *Weatherford, OK*

Santa in Vietnam

Troops bring an American Christmas to war orphans.

3

1

2

OUTSIDE SAIGON, 1967

While serving with the 222nd Combat Aviation Battalion near the city of Vung Tau, Vietnam, Edwin Lloyd Jr. and his fellow servicemen threw a Christmas party for a local orphanage. For the children, it was their first time meeting Santa Claus, who arrived via chopper. For Edwin and his troop-elves, it remains a joyful memory from an otherwise tough time.

1: *Santa (Edwin) strolls across the tarmac as kids marvel at his outfit. He almost lost his cotton whiskers during the windy ride in the chopper.*
2: *Several busloads of excited kids travel from the orphanage.*
3: *Edwin waits for a pillow to fill out his Santa suit.*
4: *The children perform a dance for the base.*
5: *The festivities included a traditional feast, with roast turkey and sides.*

4

5

CHUBBY THE DREIDEL

It turned them around on the holiday in a big way.

When my boys, Marc and Eric, were growing up in the late 1970s, we lived in a neighborhood of Jews and Christians in a suburb north of New York. It was a few dozen split-level houses on a dead-end street. With so little traffic, kids played outside, making no distinction between their front yards and the road. Parents socialized as the kids played. Many of us became close friends. Chanukah (also spelled Hanukkah) and Christmas saw a merry mingling of Jewish and Christian families gathering to celebrate together.

Chanukah commemorates the rededication of the Jewish temple in Jerusalem around 200 B.C., when oil that was supposed to last one night lasted eight. We light a menorah for eight nights, and children play dreidel games with "gelt," foil-covered chocolate that represents the coins the Maccabees minted to mark their military victory over the Syrians.

Growing up in the Bronx, New York, my brother and I received our underwear rations for the year at Chanukah. That was our gift. Can you believe it? I don't recall if we got a pair each night or if they were presented to us in one fell swoop.

Raising my own family, I continued our Chanukah traditions—except for the underwear part. I vowed never to give my boys that as a gift.

We invited our Christian neighbors over for jelly doughnuts, potato latkes and candlelighting. Then we joined our friends at their homes to trim their Christmas trees and sing carols.

We took the boys into Manhattan to stroll the lavishly decked-out streets of Times Square and Fifth Avenue. Then we went over to Rockefeller Center to glimpse the colossal tree and admire the skaters spinning and gliding around the rink.

But that time of year can be hard on Jewish kids. Christmas is everywhere. Marc and Eric said Chanukah felt less important. That saddened me. I tried to think of a way to inject a little more funukah into Chanukah.

I decided we needed a giant dreidel.

We constructed a wire frame and plastered it in papier-mache. The process was a sticky, gooey mess, but tons of fun. When the 40-by-40-inch dreidel finally was finished and painted, the boys tried to put their arms around it.

"We can't hug it! It's too chubby."

So it was. Chubby became the focal point of our eight-night Chanukah celebrations—and the hit of the street. Everybody loved Chubby.

Our joint holiday celebrations and trips to Manhattan continued, but my boys came to see Chanukah as the best holiday ever. After all, no one else had anything like Chubby the dreidel.

It brought us many years of joy and now does the same for the next generation.

Sheryl Lindsell-Roberts • *Marlborough, MA*

ANA HARD

CHRISTMAS COMMERCE

'Tis the season for spenders.

DIE-CAST FUN

Hubley made a name in die-cast toys by having its designers attend automotive trade shows and pore through car ads to make sure their miniature versions were like the real thing. The charm in this ad is in the hint that Santa might be playing with that cute little airplane under the tree.

'54

'47

LIGHTEN UP

GE began selling Christmas lights in 1903, but at $12 a set, illuminating a whole tree was strictly a rich man's game. America wasn't fully electric until the 1940s. By then, GE's holiday lights were more affordable, as shown in this festive ad from *Life*.

Give Jolly Good Fun to Everyone

give Milton Bradley Christmas Games

This year, give the gift that makes a Christmas hit with everyone. Give a Milton Bradley *family-fun* game to every name on your gift list.

Every Milton Bradley game offers excitement . . . suspense . . . entertainment. What's more, you're always sure you're giving just the right game . . . the age level is clearly marked on the cover!

To make your Christmas shopping easier, shop this page. Pick out Milton Bradley games for your family and friends. Take this page to your favorite store, and buy the games you've selected.

Then, Christmas morning, watch all the faces light up when you give jolly good fun to everyone!

MILTON BRADLEY COMPANY SPRINGFIELD 2, MASS.
Manufactured and distributed in Canada through Somerville Industries, Ltd.
Prices slightly higher in western U.S.A. and Canada.

1 SQUARE MILE* (Ages 10-adult) New land development game unlike any other you've ever played! You start with a tract of land and $100,000 . . . shrewdest developer of residential, industrial and commercial property wins! **$7.00**

2 RACK-O* (Ages 10-adult) Plenty of excitement as you race to get numbered cards in sequence. 2, 3, or 4 can play this highly absorbing game . . . and it's even more fun with partners! **$2.00**

3 GAME OF THE STATES (Ages 7-14) Children play their way across the U.S.A. . . . and learn states, capitals, important industries and products. 2 to 4 players see who can buy and sell the most from coast to coast. **$3.00**

4 GO TO THE HEAD OF THE CLASS* (Ages 8-adult) World's favorite quiz game . . . now in 10th Edition! 2 to 8 players answer age-graded questions. Advancement depends on knowledge, ingenuity, luck. Fast-moving fun! **$3.00**

5 STRATEGO* (Ages 9-adult) Fascinating new game of skill and strategy for two players. The rank of each colorful wooden piece is hidden from opponent until attacked. Easy to learn . . . never plays the same twice. **$5.00**

6 EASY MONEY* (Ages 7-adult) The action's fast as you try to win a fortune in this popular game! 2 to 6 compete for real estate . . . run a business . . . try to win a lottery. **$2.00 or $3.00**

7 THE GAME OF LIFE* (Ages 10-adult) Like life itself, this calls for skill and luck; skill in making true-to-life decisions, luck in spinning Wheel of Fate. 2 to 8 can play this big favorite. Endorsed by Art Linkletter! **$5.00**

8 SUMMIT* (Ages 10-adult) Exciting new game of cold war strategy. 3 to 6 players apply economic, military and propaganda pressure that leads up to Summit Conference. Played on colorful world map. Action, suspense, fun! **$7.00**

*REG. U.S. PAT. OFF.

WATCH FOR MILTON BRADLEY ON THESE PROGRAMS FROM NOW 'TIL CHRISTMAS . . . McKEEVER AND THE COLONEL TENNESSEE ERNIE FORD — FATHER KNOWS BEST MAKE A FACE
SUNDAY, 6:30 P.M., NBC-TV Mon.-Fri., 12 Noon-to 1:00 P.M., ABC-TV SATURDAY, 11 A.M., ABC-TV

'62 THE NAME OF THE GAME

Of the array of board games in this fictional store window, only Stratego and The Game of Life have stood the test of time. And no small wonder, really: Easy Money is a poor man's Monopoly, and Summit is described as an "exciting new game of Cold War strategy." Square Mile has players as real estate developers that amass land for "residential, industrial and commercial property." Hmm. Better stick with a bike or Barbie, Mom.

Pictures from the Past

MEETING SANTA

THREE'S COMPANY (AND SIX IS A FAMILY)

My mother, Patricia Merwine, looks happy at Santa's knee at Lipkin's in Bethlehem in 1947. Little did she and her siblings know that three more kids would join the family. Maybe Santa knew?

Martin Di Maria
Bethlehem, PA

SMILE FOR THE CAMERA!

I'm in the center here at age 7 visiting Santa with my brother David, 9, and sister Kathy, 3, in 1976 at Camp Darby in Italy, where our dad was stationed.

Judy Oliver • *Huntsville, TX*

SPECIAL TIME

I fondly recall seeing Santa with my cousin Gerry in 1958 at the Adam, Meldrum & Anderson store in Buffalo, New York. I'm on the right. What joy we had that day!

*Mary Ann
Ladowski Goodemote*

ON THE RECORD

After telling Santa what I wanted, he asked if I got my parents anything. I told him that my sister Emma, 8, and I would give them a box of candy. I had no idea I was being recorded. When my parents played the record at home, I could be heard spilling the beans. Boy, was Emma mad at me. This was in 1950, when I was 5. I love my bangs and my Toni home perm. And I still have that recording.

Cathy Eddings • Pittsburgh, PA

QUICK STOP

My dad, Ronald, had a broken leg, but before seeing the doctor he insisted on visiting Santa at Hess Brothers in Allentown, Pennsylvania, in 1946.

Ronald Frederick Jr.

AS THE SONG SAYS, I REALLY CAN'T STAY
My daughter Kristen, 6 months, is confused, but my son Jeff, 3, was clearly unhappy that day in 1974 at the Watt & Shand store in Lancaster, Pennsylvania.

Elaine Grant • Uncasville, CT

WHAT'S ON YOUR LIST?
I love this image of my mother-in-law, Helen Davis Worthington, visiting Santa at Frederick & Nelson in Seattle, Washington, in 1945. It truly captures the surprise and magic of Christmas.

Michelle Sprague • Tonasket, WA

MASKED MAN
At 2 years old in 1940, I wasn't afraid of my dad's Santa mask. But today, it gives me chills!

Dottie Hatton Lasley • Princeton, NJ

SAY CHEESE!

My husband, Joe, left, and I didn't know each other in the early 1950s, but it looks as if our mothers had similar taste in plaid coats and took us to the same not-so-jolly-looking Santa Claus in Bethlehem, Pennsylvania. Years later, Joe and I recalled being scared of that Santa; Joe wouldn't talk to him.

I managed to ask for one thing: a Cadillac like the one my rich Uncle Larry drove. I never did get it.

Barbara Adamcik • Freemansburg, PA

NOT SURE ABOUT SANTA

Going to Lazarus Department Store in downtown Columbus with my older sister, Linda, was a great adventure in 1955—at least one whole floor was dedicated to children.

Mary Garvin • Columbus, OH

Friends saw the likenesses of Jim, Bernie and Ron on the card.

MODEL ALTAR BOYS

The story behind a Christmas card.

Sarasota, Florida, was growing in the 1950s—the city added subdivisions, shopping centers and schools—but it still had a small-town feel. My family was well known in the community: Dad was active in the Episcopal Church, where he was an administrator for several programs, and we all worked at the family retail office supply business.

Both of my parents' families had moved to Sarasota in the 1920s. Mom and Dad met in high school, but in the early 1930s, they left to find work in New York. Dad worked for the government during the war, setting up training programs in defense plants, experience that allowed him to transfer to Florida in 1942. We moved to Sarasota in early 1943.

By 1950 the city had an active art scene and was home to several well-known authors, artists and illustrators. Joseph J. Steinmetz, a professional photographer who was a family friend and customer, knew that my brother Jim and I were altar boys at church, which is how we got a unique assignment.

An artist who worked for the greeting card company Hallmark commissioned Steinmetz to take a photo for a Christmas card. With Dad's permission, one day after school, Jim, his friend Bernie Scriven and I dressed in our acolyte cassocks and modeled for a picture. The photo session took only an hour, for which we each received $25—which felt, to us, like a lot of money.

The Hallmark artist, Jerry Farnsworth, then used the photo to create an illustration that was put on a Christmas card that year.

When we saw the card in the Hallmark catalog, we were surprised at how much the boys looked like us. We got a lot of attention for it, including from our friends, who recognized us. We were generally very well-grounded kids, but we certainly felt proud of being on that card.

Those connections in Sarasota's church, business and arts communities continued to be an important part of my life: I later served two terms as mayor.

Ron Norman • San Antonio, TX

"Her presents all unwrapped and waiting to be played with,
my daughter Paula sits for a moment to let me snap a quick
picture one holiday in the '60s."

Barbara Mohr • *Millington, MI*

Let's Celebrate!

Birthdays and weddings are just two reasons the whole gang joins in the excitement. Enjoy this selection of notable special events.

FROM ROOKIE TO ROADMASTER

A shaky new relationship finds footing in a special gift.

My mother, Mary, remarried around the same time as my ninth birthday. I had a small celebration with my grandparents that day. My grandma made a luscious cake and I got some nice presents, but not the one thing that I had been asking—no, begging—for.

That week, my stepfather, Dean Hand, moved us to another state for his job, and I sulked. I missed Grandma and Grandpa, who pretty much raised me. I didn't know anyone in Sterling, Colorado, our new home. And I didn't get what I wanted for my birthday.

Our new block had many kids, mostly boys, around my age. And they all had what I craved—a bicycle. But my mother was overprotective. She thought bikes were too dangerous for girls. Luckily, the boys were very generous about letting me take a ride, which only made me want my own more.

Don't forget, bikes in the 1940s were all the same standard size. You lowered the handlebars or the seat to fit a smaller rider.

I was tall for my age, so I didn't fall off too many times. But my mother wasn't happy about the possibility of me wrecking another kid's bike.

Even though my stepfather and I often clashed that first year—my grandparents had spoiled me and he wasn't used to being a parent—he took my side on this issue. "Let the kids play," he told Mom.

With my 10th birthday soon approaching, I began to campaign hard for a bike once again. My mother continued to say no, telling me that money was scarce and that bikes were too dangerous.

What neither of us knew was that my stepfather had secretly bought one for me and hidden it at a neighbor's.

The morning I turned 10, there was a lovely blue Roadmaster with shiny chrome fenders parked right outside our front door.

That proved to be my most-remembered birthday. It also marked a turning point in my relationship with my stepdaddy. He trusted me to ride safely and showed me how to take care of my prized new possession. Later, he admitted that when he was a boy on the cattle ranch, he had never owned a bike and always longed for one.

I rode that bike for over 50 years.

Paula Cornelison • Ave Maria, FL

Birthday Wishes

My friends and me on the couch (above) at my seventh birthday is one of my favorite photos. I can't look at it without smiling. I'm third from the right.

Cheryl Morgan • *Brooklyn Park, MN*

Because my birthday is on Christmas Eve, it often gets a bit lost. The only party I ever had was when I was 7—my mom let me invite a few of my friends over for a luncheon. She made us sandwiches cut out with Christmas cookie cutters, and we drank Kool-Aid. And of course, there was cake and ice cream!

Beverly Duell-Moore

My sixth, seventh and eighth birthday parties were all held at McDonald's. I still love looking at the pictures in my scrapbook of my classmates and me eating hamburgers, cheeseburgers and fries and sitting in the booths with the '80s McDonald's decor!

Sabrina Steyling

I had several birthday parties when I was in elementary school. When I was ages 3 to 8, my mother made me the special animal cakes from the Baker's Coconut cookbook.

Cindy Fowler

BETTER THAN BIRTHDAY CAKE

Celebrating my 10th birthday on April 2, 1943, was tough. The war was on, and just about everything was rationed or impossible to get. Yet I received a really special gift that year—a tin can of pink salmon. The gift was earmarked for me because I absolutely loved salmon. I especially loved my mother's salmon patties with cream sauce and peas on top.

My mother, Gertrude, even made the package special to open. She wrapped the can in a small box and placed that box inside a larger one. Then she found four more boxes, each one slightly larger than the other, and wrapped each after the smaller box was placed inside. The excitement of opening each of those boxes with their wrappings and finally getting to the smallest package of my prized salmon made me squeal with delight.

My mother told my six sisters and two brothers that this was my treat, and that no one else was to touch it. I was generous, however, and shared.

Janet Nowicki • Buffalo, NY

Janet's sister Colleen, left, holds hands with the doll Janet received for a different birthday.

Wilma's mother, Virgie (left, in 1947), smiled when she poured cream on her cereal. She loved her birthday gift of a pig creamer (below).

Beating the Birthday Blues

Mama's birthday was coming, and I wanted to buy her something nice. Lifting her spirits on this birthday was especially important because my father had passed away just a few months before and we were all still grieving.

I'd been able to save up only 35 cents from my Saturday job at the grocery store in Mena, Arkansas, which wasn't much to buy a gift, even back in the early 1940s. But I was determined to give my mother something to make her laugh again.

The day before her birthday, I was at my job when I saw a lady opening a 35-cent box of oatmeal she'd just bought. She pulled out a sugar bowl and creamer shaped like cute little pigs.

I never thought such nice dishes could come packaged with oatmeal, and the pigs had winsome expressions that made me laugh. Maybe they would make Mama laugh, too.

Right away, I offered the customer my 35 cents in exchange for the bowl and creamer, explaining that I needed a birthday present for my mother. She cheerfully agreed to sell them to me.

By the time Mama came home from work, I had the table all set with the gift waiting. When she opened the present she laughed and said, "What cute little pigs!"

All these years later, I still have the creamer (my niece has the sugar bowl). My grandchildren use the creamer for tea parties and usually beg me to retell the story of the birthday present. As I do, I remember that it's often the little things that have lasting value.

Wilma Moody • Aurora, MO

Pictures from the Past
BIRTHDAYS

GLAMOUR GIRL

My hair is up in curlers and I'm wearing my favorite dress for grandma Lydia Dickman's birthday in August 1962. Family friend Nell is on the left next to my mom, holding Kevin, then it's Grandma and the rest of the usual cast of characters: my brothers Eric, Craig and Mark. They're dressed like they'd been working on their latest project.

Lisa Krall • *Dewey, IL*

IT MATCHES!

In June 1955, Mom went all out for my sixth birthday. She served Neapolitan ice cream with a matching Neapolitan cake. I thought she was the cleverest woman in the world.

Diane Rondo Fanelli • *Warren, MI*

JUST LIKE MOM

My mother, Emily Beatrice Pittman Walker, was a nurse and my hero. On my third birthday, in April 1957, I was proud to get a nursing bag just like hers.

Joanne Walker Clayton • *Herrin, IL*

THE PERFECT AMERICAN FAMILY

After dinner, we ran outside because there were always plenty of good kids to play with in our neighborhood. Mom and Dad worked hard to create this life for us. I am fortunate to belong to the baby boom. Elise (left) and I turned 5 in 1968. We celebrated with our sisters Carol (in green) and Judith, and our parents, Irene and Edward.

Ellen Groves Paiva
Wallingford, CT

FLUFFY FIFFY

Fiffy was my present for my 10th birthday in the spring of 1966, and then my companion for the next 11 years. That little dog was the best birthday gift ever. My sister Evelyn is sitting beside me outside our house in Prairie Village, Kansas.

Suzy Moffitt • *South Bend, IN*

RAINBOW OF DRESSES

My friends dressed in their Sunday best for my 10th birthday party in 1963. I'm on the left, then Maureen, Nancy, Ann, Colleen and Lori.

Debbie Bryant
Rocky River, OH

LITTLE COWBOY

On his third birthday, in 1961, my son Gary Michael shows off a brand-new Stetson that went with a full cowboy suit. Our family lived in Liberal, Kansas, at the time. Today, he lives in Bixby, Oklahoma, and wears a different hat as the part owner of a flight instruction school.

Marlene Barnes

WINNING DAY

I celebrated my 26th birthday in Hermann, Missouri, in 1979, after winning my way into three finals of the Jaycees Tennis Tournament. I went home with an armload of trophies (right)—the best birthday presents ever!

Glenda Ferguson • Paoli, IN

Look What the Stork Brought

Vintage birth announcements and greeting cards celebrate new arrivals. Symbols of good luck and fertility, the stork, four-leaf clover and bluebird, along with written sentiments, conveyed the hopes and ideals of the times.

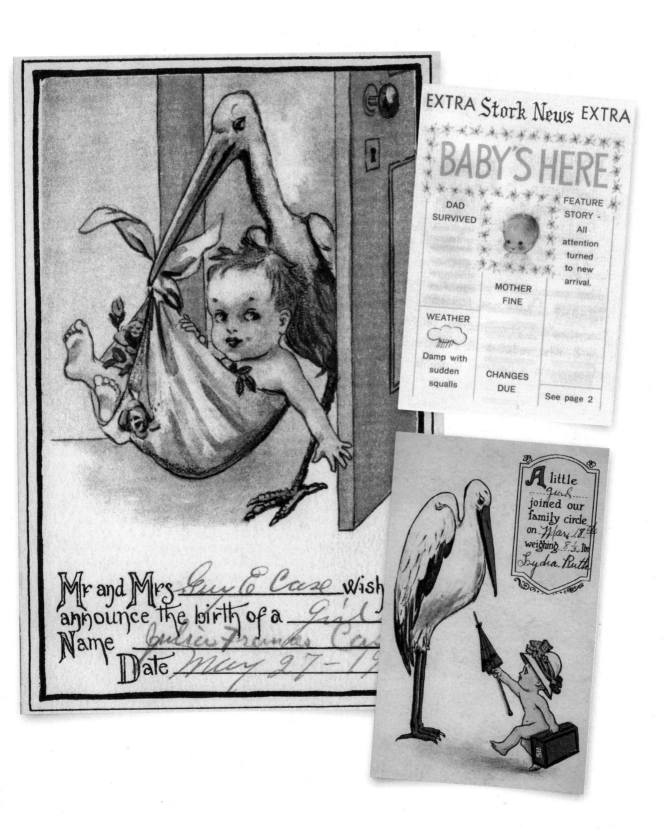

EXTRA Stork News EXTRA

BABY'S HERE

DAD SURVIVED

FEATURE STORY -
All attention turned to new arrival.

MOTHER FINE

WEATHER

Damp with sudden squalls

CHANGES DUE

See page 2

Mr and Mrs _Guy E Case_ wish
announce the birth of a _Girl_
Name _Julia Frances Case_
Date _May 27 - 19_

A little _girl_ joined our family circle on _May 18_ weighing _8¾ lbs_
Lydia Ruth

Pictures from the Past

FIRST COMMUNION

KEEPING FAITH

My twin, Norman, and I had our First Communion at Saints Peter and Paul Church in Fall River, Massachusetts, in the early 1950s.

Kathleen Timberlake Digits
Georgetown, TX

SPRING SPECIAL

In 1972, for my First Communion, all signs pointed to spring, with snow melting in the background.

Lori East Sheldon • *Borger, TX*

FITTING ATTIRE

I wore a traditional dress for my communion in 1961 in Shannon, Illinois, and my mom, Barbara, was in her Sunday best.

Kathleen Manning Weber • *Shannon, IL*

CLASSIC POSE

In 1962 a new dress, book and wristwatch marked the special occasion of my First Communion.

Lauren Majcher • *Syracuse, NY*

ALL IN WHITE

I had my First Communion in the early '60s in Germany, where my father was transferred for his job. I was only 6 or 7, but I understood it was a very solemn affair.

Phyllis Gebhardt • *Kissimmee, FL*

FIVE TIMES A BRIDE

She still fits beautifully into that hand-sewn gown.

My beautiful wife, Betty Jane Budd Griffin, has worn her original wedding gown five times in celebrating our many years of marriage together. It was created for her by a close family friend.

William E. Griffin • *Jacksonville, FL*

1: *Our wedding day, August 18, 1946. Betty is in her parents' backyard in Holt, Michigan.*
2: *In 1971, celebrating our 25th anniversary. With Betty are her mom, Julia Budd Hutcheon, and our daughters Annette Griffin Manley and Amy Griffin Monson.*
3: *In Reeve, Wisconsin, in 1986, for our 40th anniversary. We repeated our wedding vows with Pastor Les Pardun officiating.*
4: *Celebrating our 50th anniversary in 1996 in Jacksonville, Florida. Betty is with our youngest grandchild, Hannah Marie Griffin, now 24.*
5: *In 2006, our 60th anniversary at our church in Jacksonville, Florida.*

Bevy of Beauties

For the 50th wedding anniversary of my parents, Alfred and Eva Swan, on June 29, 1972, I thought it'd be fun for my sisters and me to put on our gowns, too. Mother had made her gown as well as those of her three daughters.

So my mother, my two sisters and I, and four of my mother's granddaughters dressed in our gowns (Mother is in the knee-length dress) and held a procession into the backyard.

My parents had 18 grandchildren, and with all of them and their spouses, it was great fun to have everyone sing "Here Comes the Bride." My son even took a picture from behind as a joke, which shows that some of the gowns no longer fit around the brides.

Jeanne Swan Garnett
Madison, WI

TWO SISTERS, ONE WEDDING

My twin sister, Jean, and I got married on July 11, 1964, in a double wedding ceremony. We have always enjoyed dressing alike, and for our weddings we chose identical wedding dresses, veils and bouquets.

Jean and I have been best friends forever. We even had our baby showers together—our babies were born within a month or two of each other each time we were expecting. When the children were born, Jean and I raised our babies as brothers and sisters rather than cousins.

Janet Weber • Mishawaka, IN

Twins Jean and Janet wore gowns of imported Chantilly lace and long chapel trains.

Pictures from the Past
WEDDINGS

THIRSTY?

This was on our wedding day, in 1972. I was feeling hot, and someone found us the Cokes. Charles and I were married for almost 39 years. Just like the Coke slogan said: "It's the Real Thing."

Lois Mevs • Honea Path, SC

DOUBLE UP

Just after World War II, lots of young people were anxious to get married, and if sisters were involved, why not have a double wedding? That's what my bride, Stella, and I (on the right) did on June 7, 1946, with her sister Helen and Helen's groom, Almon.

Robert P. McConnell • Hillsdale, MI

WHEN IT BEGAN

This was at Douglas College in New Jersey the day Eleanor and I married. We've celebrated more than 50 years together.

Bill Kover • *Piscataway, NJ*

FAUX PAS FROM THE START

The blunders began early for me and my first husband, Tony Chickillo. Our marriage ceremony on Nov. 22, 1969, was rife with miscues. As I walked down the aisle in my white minidress, audible gasps rose from the crowd. The minister then forgot to ask, "Who gives this woman?" That left my father in an awkward bind at the altar. To top it all off, the minister never pronounced us husband and wife or gave the groom permission to kiss the bride. Tony took care of that part himself.

Suzy Littlejohn Chickillo Hopkins
Denver, CO

THE SWEET TASTE OF SICILIAN PASTRY

My father, bakery owner Salvatore Marino, was an Italian immigrant from the island of Sicily. Here he stands near a wedding cake he has just finished decorating while his business partner Vito Aliotto looks on. I think it was likely a fruit cake, a popular choice during the early 1930s. My father used only the freshest ingredients in his baking, with no glucose or other additives. He owned two bakeries at the time, one in Monterey, the other called The Cake Box in Oakland, California.

Pietrina Di Piazza
Hayward, CA

BEST BARGAIN

My wedding dress cost a total of $4.50—fabric at $0.25 a yard, a zipper, lace for the bodice and sleeves, a pattern, thread and a dozen tiny buttons for the back of the dress. Cork and I were married Aug. 12, 1962. Now, decades later, I still have the dress and we're still married.

Rosanne Ballou • Delphos, KS

SOMETHING BLUE STUCK LIKE SOMETHING GLUE

Their wedding really went by in a flash.

A t nursing school in the 1950s, we attended classes all year long for three years. We were allowed to be engaged, but we couldn't marry until the final four months of the program.

Tony and I were to marry in mid-May, and three of my classmates had scheduled their weddings for around the same time. The four of us decided that our "something blue" would be a pretty blue garter that each woman could pass along to the next bride. I was the last in line.

I weighed 106 in those days and the women before me were all a bit heftier. So by the time it got to me, the garter was so stretched that I had to hike it up to my thigh to get it to stay in place.

My wedding dress had a hoop skirt worn with lacy pantaloons underneath, and my shoes had stylish bows. This fashion combination proved to be my undoing.

During the Mass, I stood up from kneeling and felt the garter slip down my leg. I tried kicking it loose, but it caught on the bow of my shoe.

"What's wrong?" Tony whispered. I shook my head and tried to concentrate on the ceremony.

We said our vows and kneeled again as the priest continued with the blessing. All I could think about was that garter clinging to my foot. I didn't want to walk down the aisle and have everyone see it. So I reached down to grab it—and I heard my mother catch her breath.

Tony looked at me in shock.

"What the hell are you doing?!" he asked.

"Trying to get this garter off my shoe," I whispered back.

"You're pushing up your hoop skirt in the back now and showing everyone those cute panties."

Suddenly, the thought of our guests seeing the little blue garter didn't seem so bad by comparison. Unfortunately, my troubles weren't over.

Following tradition, I took a few of the flowers from the wedding bouquet to place in front of the Virgin Mary. Determined to keep the garter hidden as I walked to the statue, I nearly fell—

twice—when I stepped on the hem of my dress. The entire congregation seemed to gasp with each near miss. By this point, I hated that darn garter.

Finally, leaving the church, I lifted my skirt and kicked the thing as far from me as possible. When he saw me do that, Tony knew he was in for an interesting life.

We've now celebrated many happy years together.

Marge Dodero • Seal Beach, CA

"We were high school sweethearts in the '60s. I designed and
made my gown from imported Dutch satin. My veil attached
to a cabbage-rose headpiece. Our special day was
November 30, 1963, and every day since is still special."

Trudy Zurmely • Junction City, KS